Ad Lib
A Sojourn Impromptu

Richard L. Taylor, FAIA

Europe Through an Architect's Eye

A D L I B
ad 'lib/*verb*

synonyms: make it up as one goes along, wing it

Ad Lib
A Sojourn Impromptu

Copyright © 2018 by Richard L. Taylor, Jr., FAIA

All rights reserved. No part of this book may be reproduced or transmitted in any form or by any means without written permission of the author.

ISBN   978-0-9987528-9-1

Library of Congress Control Number: 2017934798

Published by:
Full Quark Press
Atlanta, GA

This journal records a make-it-up-as-you-go-along excursion to Europe in the spring of 2017.

All of the images presented were shot with the photo feature of a standard iPhone 6.

Travel agenda: Two people too busy to do much planning, two bags, two weeks, two thousand euros in a money belt, and two round-trip tickets: ATL—CDG—ATL

Why Paris?

Because Nancy remarked one time, "Oh, Paris? I've never been there."

One caveat: hotel reservations were confirmed for the first night only. (Yeah, I know. But we're old!) After that, Europe is our oyster.

DAYS & DESTINATIONS

Contents

1	Atlanta	1
2	Paris	7
3	Paris	25
4	Paris	39
5	Paris	45
6	Paris to Barcelona	53
7	Barcelona	61
8	Barcelona	73
9	The Mediterranean Sea	81
10	Civitavecchia—Rome	89
11	Rome	97
12	Roma	109
13	Rome to Florence	125
14	Florence to Venice	133
15	Venice	137
16	Venice to Paris	145
17	Paris to Atlanta	151

 DAY 1
Atlanta

5:17 p.m. ATL, GA

Two hundred years ago, William Wordsworth wrote, "The world is too much with us, Milton, coming and going, early and late, getting and spending." Or something like that. This was penned before Peter Cooper invented the first American-built steam locomotive (called *Tom Thumb*) or the first coil-spring alarm clock was wound up.

Few would argue that our contemporary tempo of life has done much to improve the situation.

This evening, soothed with music in one ear, and intimidated with safety warnings in the other, Mitch and I sit inside Atlanta's glitzy twenty-first-century international airport. Occasionally, alarms buzz. Sporadically, an electronic accent will render cryptic instructions to travelers who are either stoically anaesthetized or nervously herded through to some destination—*early and late.*

Since we are an hour ahead of schedule, we sit, shoulder to shoulder, in the *stoically anaesthetized* section, patiently waiting to board a night flight to Paris, France, *coming and going.*

After forty-four years of uninterrupted marital bliss, this is our first trip for just the two of us. Part of the "bliss-package," as you might expect, includes raising housecats that shed, dogs that bark but don't bite, generations of rodents who multiply with great prodigiously, and three exceptional children—now grown, educated, married and moved out. Each variety of house species turned out bright, beautiful, healthy, and rambunctious. Our current project is working on three grandsons. Every early indicator is at the top of the green. The other part of the bliss thing is, let's say, somewhat self-illusionary—no one can see it but us.

And I ain't touching that one.

"Mitch" is short for Mitchell, Nancy's maiden surname. Along the way I've tried chummier endearments, but so far, Mitch just seems to fit. It's polite, personal, and to the point. As far as I know, she's "Nancy" to everybody else.

Thirty minutes ago, she and I negotiated our way through airport security. Shakedowns are always annoying, but as seniors (Mitch is seventy-five, and I'm eighty-one), we don't have to take our shoes off. Thank you, TSA, for one small, demonstration of judgment.

So how does this belated *grand-tour* commence this evening? First off, Mitch has been on her cell phone for the last thirty minutes with her favorite telephone buddy, our son, Richard (III). If Sir Isaac Newton was correct, this motion will stay in motion until disturbed by some outside force. In their case, a tornado might not do it, but a slight wind shift might. Apparently *the parent's* personal stuff will simply have to wait for the last drip from the family tree to drop. So what's new?

Now, since I just mentioned Richard by name, Mitch tells me that I have to also mention the girls. Hence: Lee is our firstborn and is a classical violinist. Ruthie, our youngest, is a fire-breathing environmentalist. Just to complete the sketch, Mitch is an interior designer with her own firm, and Richard and I are both architects. And, no, he doesn't work for me. We tried it, but he wanted to be boss. But that's an old story that goes back to biblical times and doesn't need repeating.

So there! Now you know all you need to know about how to achieve the marital-bliss status mentioned above: JDWYTADIN (*Just do what you're told and do it now*).

Before we get started, let me make a few quick comments about journal-keeping. First off, good or bad, it is a long-standing habit of mine. I have a bookshelf of them. Perhaps they are compensation for an imperfect memory. Secondly, you'll see I've included the cost of many of the expenses incurred along the way. To some, this may feel like bad manners. But to me, prices are just reference points that, when looked at a hundred years from now, will be interesting. Anyone know what a minié ball cost in 1776? I do. Lafayette noted it in a journal.

Keeping a journal, by its very nature, will record *how* one see things. Photographs (or sketches– in Lafayette's case) will record *what* you see. Both are good, but there is a significant difference. Photographs record the surface of things. The written word records an interpretation of things.

Is one way superior to the other? I don't know. But Socrates had a way of answering tough choices. With hemlock in hand, he said, "Which is better, God only knows."

Well, that's good enough for me

By the way (off subject and before I forget it), the exchange rate between currencies in March 2017, averaged one euro to about 1.25 USD.

We board our plane at 6:45, and the captain tucks the wheels in the wells at 7:30 p.m. EST. It's now 2:15 a.m. EST. According to the little flat screen on the back of the seat in front of me, we have now stepped up to an altitude of thirty-two thousand feet. The Great Circle Route takes us right up the east coast of the States and then out to sea somewhere south of Boston. We're now cruising along nicely over the mid-Atlantic. The southern tip of Greenland should be just aft of our left wingtip.

The plane is not the rigid aluminum bird it looks like. Even in moderate bumps, it flexes and undulates. Dinner, four hours ago, was pre-packaged everything—baked chicken, applesauce, rice, water-in-a-sealed-cup and a slice of pound cake. In terms of quality and variety, it beats the daylights out of MREs (military Meals Ready to Eat).

Mitch and I are still sitting shoulder to shoulder, but this time in a packed-to-the-brim Boeing 777 wide-body. Our seats are about amid-ship and next to the central toilets and service modules. This location gives us a window on one side and the aisle on the other—and no neighbors to try to get along with. I'm on the aisle. Potty-runs are a snap. This is almost a little like luxury. However, the size of one's personal space is a constant reminder of the prevailing class distinctions. Our seating arrangement feels more like privileged lower-class than tourist. For us, this is fine. We all live in the economic world we fancy we live in anyway. Isn't that true?

Mitch's porthole to the outside world looks due south over the Atlantic Ocean. The layer of broken clouds below goes out to a distant and faint horizon. Stars and planets are barely visible because of the sun's glaring reflection off an almost full-moon. The stars we can see are all to the east—toward Europe.

Except for the high-pitched whine of the big GE turbofans, the interior of the cabin is quiet as a morgue and just about as dark. There are hundreds of shadowy bodies in here; all movements look like ghost profiles and seem to be in slow motion.

Still on post on starboard watch, Mitch is intent on keeping track of the escaping moon and its flickering reflection off the ocean surface as it glitters off and on between the broken cloud-deck below.

Those passengers up front, the ones with all the comfy legroom and free adult beverages, are located above the broad wing roots and cannot see the full glory of the universe in night's bloom. They can only see from the horizon up. But is that not the way it has always been for the privileged few—and will always be—and maybe the way it's supposed to be? Ms. Antoinette had the answer: "Let 'em eat cake."

Ad Lib

Somewhere, in the course of a brief nod off, today turned into yesterday, and it's already tomorrow. Or is it, yesterday turned into today. Hmm, works both ways.

 DAY 2
Paris

Any way you slice it, it's still a long night, and the sun has not yet made its morning debut. Mitch catches maybe an hour's sleep, probably less. From her waist-gunner position, she still continues to give thirty-minute position reports on the progress of the waning moon. When it finally does fade behind our vapor trail, the night definitely gets a little longer—and a little darker.

Periodically, she looks over at me and says with a half-smile, "It's still undercast." I think I'm supposed to marvel at her inventive meteorological terminology.

As I say, there is not much going on, either outside or inside the plane. Most of the passengers are feigning sleep, but a few are reading. Thankfully, any talking going on is being done softly.

Mitch and I are both licensed pilots and have been flying for years, so riding here in the back seat is not our norm.

Right now, I think about the two guys sitting in the glow of the instrument lights in the cockpit up front. They have plenty to think about, and not all of it has to do with flying.

You do know what they say about flying, don't you? "Hours and hours of idle boredom interrupted by moments of sheer terror." Well, even though this is not exactly true, there is a message in there somewhere. In any event, pilots don't need to talk much when they are daydreaming. Probably, right now, they're just monitoring the autopilot and occasionally radioing position reports. I remember, longingly, how creatively detached one's mind can become on long-haul night flights. The mind image is like one of those rare dreams you remember in precise detail while forgetting the story line.

When flying, you are alert and focused, but you are still curled up in your own brain box and just peeking out. All of the there-I-was-at-thirty-thousand-with-one-turning-and-one-burning stories of derring-do can wait for spool-down time with a dewy-eyed audience in a dark bar. Right now, in heaven's bosom, it's spiritual time. All pilots respect that.

Here in the cargo hold, the flight is nothing but long and boring. On the other hand, think about what a luxury it is to be cruising along effortlessly at 550 miles per hour over the middle of the Atlantic Ocean—and bored! So please understand, I'm not complaining. My sincerest feeling is just the opposite. I am grateful to the extreme. This particular kind of boredom is a privilege of unparalleled magnitude. It is magic, undreamed of throughout history. And we take it for granted—even bitch about it!

But it's still boring. And I'm still luxuriating in it.

After nearly eight hours of night flight, here comes the sun. It arrives in full blossom just as we touch down at Charles de Gaulle International at 7:34 a.m., local. What a perfect morning—clear, blue sky, 50°F. The air feels fresh with fully charged particles of pure, unprocessed oxygen.

When we were checking in at the ticket counter in Atlanta, as end-of-the-line, non-SkyMiles passengers, a rather testy Delta agent told me that my carry-on bag was too big for the overhead bin. I put it in the demonstration frame they provided, and it fit, albeit snugly. She still insisted that it had to be categorized as "checked luggage."

Of course our plan was to have no *luggage* to fool with, only two overhead bags on little wheels. Nice and simple. So now, upon arrival at our destination, we have the challenge of finding Baggage Claim somewhere here in bowels of the Old World. This airport (CDG) is an intimidating, institutional, work-in-progress facility operated in foreign tongue. Suddenly the morning bustle doesn't feel all that invigorating anymore. And the oxygen needle just dropped down to *stale and recycled* zone.

Like cattle, we faithfully file into the confusion of CDG. Eventually we figure out that to get to Baggage Claim we have to take an airport shuttle train to another terminal. Eventually we find the train that we think will get us there. It does not. So we have to catch a return train to our original arrival gate to start over. We reread all the directional signs and discover that the first train we took really was the correct one, but we had gotten off one stop too early. We then get back on the next train and exit at Terminal M. This time it works!

The visceral satisfaction of getting my one overhead bag back is way out of proportion to the meager scale of accomplishment. But so what? It still feels good. More importantly, I'm finally starting to get the rhythm of things. It's an empowering feeling.

Next: Customs Inspection. Of course, neither of us can read the French directional signs, nor can we understand the heavily accented woman on the over-amplified PA system. Consequently, we get in the wrong queue for passport check-in. It turns out to be a very long and slow-moving line exclusively for checking French passports. Forget my previous comment about rhythm.

Of course, we've already been in line for twenty minutes, and we're halfway to the passport window. Not wanting to lose our time-investment, we risk spending more time in the wrong line in the hope that the checker will show some mercy. Well, we get there, and she does. As a matter fact, the young lady at the window smiles and is polite and friendly almost to the extreme. She thinks it's funny what we've done and welcomes us to France quite properly. *Viva la France!* I like this place already. Positive energy comes flowing back.

We're now officially *here* and through Customs and ready to take on the task of finding Paris. It's gotta be out there somewhere. I know because we saw it glimmering through the golden, hazy dawn while we were on the final approach.

While I'm looking everywhere for big regional train maps on the airport walls, Mitch simply walks up to a tourist counter and buys two train tickets on the Metro to Paris ($12.50 each).

Now to find the train. It can't be that hard, can it?

We start the search, but the entire Metro train operation is partially obscured from the everyday airport processes by a clutter of new construction barrier walls blocking off circulation everywhere. This doesn't help things.

So Ms. Take-Charge again walks up to the first person she sees in uniform and, in her most engaging English, asks, "Which train goes to Paris?" I have yet to hear her call it Parée once. I stand to the side like the obedient porter I am—just holding the bags (as they say). Once again, machismo pales in the shadow of a determined woman.

With only a wave of a hand to direct us to the trains, we weave our way through crowds of people going in the opposite direction. Maybe this is the discharge load of a freshly arrived train. But the big clue comes when we go around a corner and find dozens of railroad cars that smell of spent electrical energy.

Our train turns out to be nice, but not fancy. It is clean, reasonably quiet, and has lots of big windows. The seats are mostly occupied, but luckily, we get a bench to ourselves facing the direction of travel (two nice qualities). Of course, the train also turns out to be a local. It stops every few minutes providing us with plenty of time to get a real sense of the working class burbs of Paris. It shows an industrial side of the city that most of us give little thought to. But who knows? Industry may be the lifeblood of culture after all.

The day is still just getting started, so there are lots of folks getting on and off along the way. And everybody is hustling. The sky stays crystal blue, and the sun is gaining altitude without even trying. We're in no hurry, and we just sightsee our way to town. I wouldn't say we are actually relaxing yet, but at least we are settled and comfortable—and going somewhere.

The street maps Mitch picked up at the airport and the diagrammatic transit schematics on the walls of the train are impossible for the average American to match up. Obviously, you have to have more information to make them jibe. Our goal is to get off the train at the Notre-Dame Cathedral. Or, as Mitch is want to say, Noder D'aim. Her Notre-Dame sounds very much like a big university in Indiana. But no matter how you pronounce it, for us the cathedral will become the focal point for our adventures in the city.

My sense is that once we get to the cathedral, we will have finally arrived in Paris. From that point we can then plan our next destination. The idea of simply hailing a taxi from the airport to the cathedral, or to the hotel, is never discussed. For some reason, using local trains seems unavoidably appropriate. Sure, there is uncertainty and challenge in

PARIS

this unknown, but it is still early in the day. We have plenty of time to figure out whatever needs figuring out.

Sightseeing from the train is interesting, but we both keep our eyes focused on terminal names. When we see the first sign with Notre-Dame (France, not Indiana) on the wall, we get off. It turns out to be the stop just before the *real* Notre-Dame Station. Realizing our mistake, we duck back into the station, catch the next train, and take it one more click. This time it works! Exiting the train platform area, like many subway systems, the one-way people-control system has a tall, revolving, interlaced, iron-pipe gate. They are like giant, blunt, vertical bread slicers. Being in charge of both of our suitcases, naturally, I get one of them caught in the slicers. This is another one of those little panic moments. By yanking and jerking desperately, I manage to muscle it out. I think an alarm went off, but I was too engaged to be sure. That was a close one.

Next, there is a long walk through the dimly lit subway tunnel. At the far end, we climb several flights of stairs out of the underworld and into the bright sunlight and the bustling street-smells of the world's most beloved city. Yes, it's just like the postcards. Human hustle is everywhere. And visible only a block away is the apse end of the cathedral. We are dead center in the heart of the Left Bank. I can hear daughter Ruthie all the way from Atlanta saying, "Woo woo!" We just stand here like the tourists we are and let all the busy people swirl around us. They don't even know we are here!

I cannot resist the urge to go straight to the cathedral. But Miss Nancy states firmly that she wants to go to the hotel first. No, I don't ask why.

Our street maps are composed more of fancy artwork than data, but our hotel appears to be about a mile west of our current location. The maps have street names that are frequently hidden under artistically sketched, thumbnail drawings of prominent buildings. Once more, we could just hail a taxi to the hotel and be done with it, but the energy in the air nixes the very thought.

It's a long mile pulling the two overhead bags on their tiny, clickity-click wheels, but in no way unpleasant. Mitch puts her purse in one of the two carry-on bags slung from her shoulders, cross-bandolier style. All the way up the Boulevard Saint-Germain, we process crusty, old beauty and nouveau novelty with every breath. We're registering five-hundred-year-old street names engraved on building cornerstones. Then right next to them are one-day-old leaf buds on the trees. Paris is both very old and very new. But everything is new to us. As we pass a Metro station that discharges up to the sidewalk, the underground air is expelled to the street. Whether it's the cork from a bottle of fine wine or a loaf of stale bread, you just gotta sniff it first. It's just what we're programmed to do.

The Hotel L'Abby is a block off of Rue de Rennes and a couple of blocks north of the Luxemburg Gardens. At first blush, other than the classically designed wrought iron gate, the hotel does not appear particularly exceptional. My guess is that this design is best described as a form of Regency style with overtones of Baroque. Or maybe it's the other way around. Entering the small but elegant courtyard starts to hint of upscale. But it is the gracious "Welcome, Monsieur and Madam" at the front door that gives it away. French

PARIS

HOTEL L'ABBY

class doesn't come on like a klaxon. It's more like the warm glow you get from a sip of brandy.

It takes a little bit of time to absorb everything in the interior design. But we do. Every detail is carefully thought out. Nothing is left to chance. The comfortable but traditional furniture, the original paintings, the wall coverings, and the healthy interior plantings are all flawlessly harmonious. And, of course, the whole place is clean as a pin, and nothing is out of place. Somehow, the interior is still warm, comfortable, and inviting.

But it's the proper, middle-aged gentleman behind the counter who finishes off the picture. He looks relaxed in his almost frumpy coat and tie, but his manner is friendly, respectful, and gracious. With his rimless glasses worn halfway down his nose, he reminds you of the approachable professor who really likes his students. There's neither condescension nor servitude in his manner; still, somehow, he remains intellectually elevated. And when he smiles, he is also serious. On top of that, something in his manner makes you feel important. He's in control, yet not the least bit controlling. Very few of us ever get to this level of *gentleman*.

It's four or five hours before check-in time, but we're still shown to our room like we're the first cousins of the owner.

Our friend, Josh Thorpe, stayed here last year with his daughter, Maddi, and they recommended it to us. The rate is $275 night, which feels to be on the upper end of our budget. But we really don't know what our budget is yet. The subject has not been brought up between us. But in this case, our first day in Europe, the quality of these accommodations is well worth almost any indulgence. As it will turn out, in a couple of weeks, we'll be quite happy to come back here again. Mitch loves the place. She nestles in like a family house cat. If you want to see somebody really light up, ask her about the fresh French bread with just a smear of warm crème cheese they serve at breakfast.

After a much needed, twenty-minute nap, we capitulate on our principles, and hail a taxi back to Notre-Dame. I'm simply way more anxious to see the cathedral than to learn about the Metro system. The train experience can wait.

Once at the cathedral, we take our position at the end of a two-hundred-foot-long ticket line. It moves along pretty well, and it takes about thirty minutes to get us in the front door.

Inside the church, the space is vaulted and lit like the eternal soul of an exulted saint. I feel drugged. My rather tired and jet-lagged old brain simply cannot grasp it all. I just want to sit down and absorb. Actually, I'd like to stretch out on the floor, put my head on a kneeler, and simply look up and breathe deeply. But I resist. Mitch is still scouting around the nave and finds that there is a guided tour, outside, *in English,* that starts at 2:00 p.m. It's now 1:50, so we hustle to find it. A stylish, sixtyish woman, trim with short, dyed-brown hair and a French/London accent is running the show. She looks very professional. The tour, we are told, costs nothing.

Our guide leads us back outside to the great plaza in front of the cathedral and immediately starts holding forth. She is a mile-a-minute talker—authoritative and knowledgeable. As a seasoned tour guide controlling a crowd, she unifies the group with engaging questions like, "Who knows the difference between a cathedral and a church?"

I think to myself about a cathedral being a building and a church being a gathering of people for worship, maybe in a field or under a tree. I disagree with her explanation,

NOTRE-DAME

but fortunately, this time I keep my mouth shut. My big-mouth *faux pas* will have to wait. (But how 'bout that French, already?)

Wait? But not for very long. Before we even reenter the cathedral, I get caught up in the excitement of the architecture and offer to explain the fundamental structural characteristics between different forms of Gothic architecture and how it grew out of traditional Romanesque design. Obviously, architectural evolution may not be of interest to the general tourist population. But it must have at least some value to some people. Think about how empowering it is for the group to see the progression of man's creativity right before their eyes. Our guide may or may not have known the difference between thick, load-bearing walls with few windows, as opposed to light, point-load structure with expanses of glass—and then the ultimate bracing contributions of flying buttresses. But she does now.

With her experience with feckless hecklers, she pretty much takes my mini-lecture in stride. And that's okay. I said my piece and should have learned my lesson. But unfortunately, I'm not done yet. Hang on. It won't take long before I step in it again.

Our guide's litany continues fast and to the point. She takes us from one of the three, grand, arched coves on the front façade (the Father, Son, and Holy Spirit) to the next, each with a rich explanation of every symbolism. She is a fountain of spiritual explanation. I am sucking it up like a Shop-Vac. As we reenter the cathedral, in the time-worn tradition, she respectfully covers her head with a black shawl and guides us to the transepts and apse of the cathedral to finish off the history lessons. At the choir, she takes the historical litany up to and through Napoleon's crowning.

As she finishes, she does not, however, mention the most interesting historical fact—that Napoleon Bonaparte took the crown right out of the Pope's hands and then crowned himself!

This is secular history, of course, not liturgical. I've already stepped out of bounds once today, but I can't help myself. I cautiously bring up this subject of the crown and the Pope. She gets incredibly apologetic and says she forgot to mention the incident. Then she goes through the whole crown-event in minute detail. It takes a full five minutes, and I feel terrible. Just a thirty-second couple of sentences would suffice.

My excuse for butting in, at least to myself, is that I'm tired, hyped, jet-lagged, and main-lining on straight adrenaline. But, still, there is never a good excuse for bad manners. And, especially, when it comes to not keeping one's big yapper shut. I wonder how you say *that* in French.

As hard as it is to believe, I'm not done yet. There's deeper doo-doo to step in.

At the end of the tour, when the group splits up, I make it a point to hang around. Then, as our guide is leaving, as inconspicuously as I know how, I go up to her alone and make *strike three*. Respectfully, and I hope generously, I offer her a carefully folded twenty-euro note as a service gratuity. It is folded so as to not show the amount. This donation, obviously, is to mitigate my guilt for strikes one and two.

She says, politely but coolly, "No, thank you, sir. I am just a volunteer." She's staring at me, wide-eyed like an owl sizing up a mouse.

I'm skeptical. She could drop the note in the donation box, if she wanted. Obviously she still smarts because I have tainted her Mother Superior image. She is not even remotely interested in offering absolution to this wayward son. And forget about trying to buy her grace. Just ain't gonna happen!

Let's hear it again for the Ugly American Comes to Paris!

On the other hand, I'm sure she would be pleased to know that I am still doing perpetual penitence for my sin—and probably will forever. I lie here before thee, prostrate and pleading, "I apologize."

Mitch, looking over my shoulder, just rolled her eyes.

Leaving the cathedral, we walk over the southerly bridge over the Seine. A twenty-something American guy with a black cowboy hat is strumming his guitar and singing country-and-western songs over a too-loud amplifier. It's hokey as all hell, and he is not very good. But it doesn't seem to bother anybody walking by the least little bit.

And *he* doesn't even have to apologize.

It's 5:00 p.m., and we haven't eaten since the 6:30, pre-landing, airline breakfast on the 777. Neither of us is really hungry, but both sense our metabolism shifting from regular fuel to nervous energy. We keep walking for another half an hour through tons of traffic, people, motorcycles, taxis, and even more people until we get to the Luxembourg Gardens.

Approaching from the street, it is walled-in with a high fence. But once inside the gates, it explodes into a wonderland of landscaped elegance. The extraordinary beauty of this spring day only adds to the magic.

The size of the park feels on the scale of Central Park in New York. There are never-ending clusters of great trees, generous lakes, gardens, squirrels, thousands of people, and a million kids. The air temp is right at 70°F, sunny, and still clear with a deep-blue sky you can only find in Photoshop or *National Geographic*.

You can't help but appreciate this visceral spectacle. The trees are just starting to bud, and Parisians by the bucket load are out sucking up sunshine. The melody and lyrics of "I Love Paris in the Springtime" are inescapable.

At the north end of the park, we walk past the French Senate. This is the granddaddy of all elegant and intimidating government buildings. As we work our way westward,

THE LUXEMBOURG GARDENS

we stop to watch a chess tournament. There are at least fifty games going on. Two guys, student types, are playing at the rate of one move per second. Maybe it's some form of speed-chess. It's so incomprehensible that I feel like I'm trying to figure out sleight of hand tricks. To move a knight and hit the timer in a second is hard to do even if you're not thinking. There's got to be a gimmick in there somewhere. But probably not.

On the way back to the hotel, we stop for dinner at a sidewalk café, the Café Cassette. Both of us are almost too hungry to sit down and eat. At first, we sit outside at a small sidewalk table, but the secondhand smoke drives us indoors. We're assigned a very nice waiter who speaks English well, but cautiously. Mitch orders a salad with chicken, and I have fish and chips. They are both good meals—very much as if we had ordered them at Manuel's Tavern in Atlanta. When I try to pay the forty-five-dollar tab, I write in a 20 percent tip. My insistence turns into a small hassle, but eventually, I prevail. Mitch discovers later, in a tourist guide, that tips are included in restaurant tabs. Oh well. That was only a ten-dollar lesson.

After leaving the restaurant, we walk the few blocks to the hotel and at 7:30 p.m., we crash. And I mean big time. Within three minutes of my closing the door to the room, Mitch is asleep, fully clothed. I stay awake another two and a half minutes so I can brush my teeth and get undressed.

As first days go, this one must be rated right up there at the top.

PARIS

THE LUXEMBOURG GARDENS

DAY 3
PARIS

My first journal entry of the morning: "Last night, M. had an embarrassing event. She said that in the middle of the night the room was so dark that she couldn't find the bathroom and peed in her pants on the way to the potty. When she told me what happened, she laughed about it. Then she said that I dare not put it in this journal; so I won't."

It was already written.

But now that I think about it, I believe that it is a little episode of some significance to this trip. On the surface it says that we are a long way from the well-worn and practiced humdrum of home life. But the bigger message in this small embarrassment is that Mitch *shared it with me*. This little intimacy never would have happened in Atlanta. On the home front, we are two well-oiled machines, each with clear and specific duties. We have separate businesses and personal checking accounts. She pays some household and family things, and I pay others. Our "sharing moments" primarily consist of addressing issues of family and professional consequence—hardly ever money and never personal foibles. However weird or unconventional this separation of responsibilities might sound, for us, it works.

So, forgive me, Mitch, for spilling the beans about the room being so dark. All in all, however, it was a wonderful little embarrassment made important only by sharing it.

We sleep in and don't get downstairs to breakfast until 9:30 a.m. Four or five tables are set up in a greenhouse extension from the original dining room. The glass-greenhouse type of enclosure protrudes unobtrusively into an interior atrium of the hotel. The tables are set to perfection: crisp, white tablecloths, polished silverware, crystal-clear glassware, and luscious green plants in the garden. The aromatic coffee comes with heated cream. The croissant pastries are pungent and delicious. As I said, Mitch strongly favors the French bread with just a hint of the crème cheese. Personally, I go for the sugary and gooey things. This is refined living at its unassuming best. After finishing our meal, we pull out a city map and start planning destinations and itineraries for the day. I can tell you right now, our itinerary is going to be nothing less than spectacular.

First on today's action plan is to take a taxi to our farthest destination, the Arch de Triumph. When we arrive there, there is so much traffic zooming around the circle of the Arch, that to get to the monument itself, you have to go down through a pedestrian tunnel system under the Champs-Élysées. Once you resurface back on the circle

NOTRE-DAME SOUTH TRANSEPT

under the great monument, you're surrounded by a merry-go-round of cars, busses, motorcycles, and trucks. The street traffic is a swirling, moving, impenetrable force. We're in the black hole of a spiral galaxy. The entire universe revolves around us at a frantic rate. Time stops. But unlike a true black hole, you can see out. The cityscape profile of Paris is the 360-degree horizon.

Well, not all time stops either. After thirty minutes of reading plaques, signs, and maps on the walls, our cultural appetite for the Mother of all Monuments is sated. We then weave our way back through the tunnel and join

THE ARCH OF TRIUMPH

the pedestrian and canine parade flowing lazily down the Champs Élysées toward the Louvre.

I can recall old movies of the Nazis parading along the Champs in 1940. A pretty gloomy day. Nobody was smiling. It's nicer to remember the Allied Forces, including Charles de Gaulle, strutting the Champs in August 1944. And all the pretty French girls laughing and kissing the Yanks.

Paris

The sidewalks along the Champs are sixty feet wide on each side of the six- or eight-lane main boulevard. It's huge. Great trees, more people, never-ending construction sites, and leashed dogs sniffing everything provide plenty of company. Just killing time as we're walking, I tell Mitch about an architectural design I worked on forty-five years ago with Rich Seedorf, a fellow teaching-colleague from Georgia Tech.

The project was to convert an old storefront building on the Champs into a series of stacked restaurants. The anchor restaurant was the Hippopotamus. Rich and I were both young design profs and collaboration was *in* in those days. The final project was clearly his design, not mine, but I did put a few fingerprints on it. Those were exciting years. Could it possibly still be here?

Halfway down the Champs, I spot the building! But it has been just recently remodeled into a Citroen auto showroom. We go inside, and they verify that it was previously

THE FORMER HIPPOPOTAMUS RESTAURANT

a Hippopotamus restaurant. To me, at least, this is exciting even though any trace of Rich's talent (or my fingerprints) has now all been washed down the Seine.

We walk farther on down the Champs to the Paris Ferris Wheel and then over to the Louvre. At the west entrance of the museum sits the I. M. Pei glass pyramid. Of course, like many old-school curmudgeons, I don't fully appreciate the architectural geometric intrusion, but that's a different story entirely. For this journal, I want Mitch to take a snapshot of me standing with my finger appearing to be on the

CHARLES DE GAULLE STILL STRUTTING THE CHAMPS, PARIS

pinnacle of the glass structure. To do this, I have to get up on a two-foot-high, concrete pylon that is about a foot square.

But as I step up on it, I lose my balance and do a PLF. For you civvie types, a PLF is the old army airborne acronym for *parachute-landing-fall*. When you hit the ground in a military jump, to dissipate energy, as soon as your feet hit dirt, you roll your legs up and over one shoulder and then land again on your feet.

Well, maybe my fall here at the Louvre is not as elegant as all that. But seeing my clumsy plight, a spry teenager rushes over to help this old man get up. I tell her I'm fine, but ask her to stand right there so I can use her as a point-of-balance to get Humpty Dumpty back up again.

Mitch just stands there, camera in hand, watching the whole thing like it's some kind of circus clown act. But when I do get back up on the pier, she takes the perfect picture. I'm sorry, but I am still new at this *getting old* thing.

We go ahead and "do the Louvre" for three intense and strenuous hours. But as my mother used to say, this is only *a lick and a promise*. We covered perhaps 20 percent of the exhibition. Maybe less. Of course, we see Mona. Everybody's gotta do that. But what really knocks our socks off is Jacques-Louis David. We both know his work by photographs, but it is embarrassing to say that neither one of us knows him by name. Seeing his paintings in full scale is a whole new and wonderful experience. What a breathtaking talent. The scale of his work is staggering. The detail, especially up close, is flawless. And the overall composition, even when viewed from the farthest corner of the gallery, is unimpeachable.

"CUTTIN' THE FOOL" AT THE LOUVRE

JACQUES-LOUIS DAVID

Three hours of raw awe and bustling crowds is all we can take, so we head back outside to wait in the grand courtyard for an open-air sightseeing bus. The spring weather holds fair with light cirrus clouds and crisp air. On the park bench next to us, we meet two women from north Georgia. They are empty-nester, matronly moms on an escape program from their husbands who don't like to travel. What a pleasure it is to sit for a bit with these two, very nice, open, friendly women.

The sightseeing bus picks us up and weaves west to the Eiffel Tower. The old-fashioned tour guide with a loudspeaker has been replaced with an earphone setup you simply plug into a panel on the seat in front of you. There's no guide for me to interrupt and correct how to tell her story. It's all one-way information. Years ago, at different colleges, Mitch and I both had to take those tedious, pre-PowerPoint lectures called *History of Architecture 101*. Today, at the foot of the Eiffel Tower looking up, some of those seeds planted so long ago are finally getting their first good watering in direct sunlight.

They didn't mention this in school, but there are a number of ways to look at Architecture. I like to start with the architect.

In a nutshell, Gustave Eiffel was born in Dijon, France in 1832, as Alexandre Gustave Bonickhausen. He switched to the catchier, *Frenchie* name when he was 48 years old. Forty three years later, right at the height of Marxism and the Jazz Age, he died at 88.

In school, his baccalaureate degree was in chemistry; however he seemed to excel in just about any academic

AN STRUCTURAL WEB OF ELEGANT BEAUTY

undertaking put before him. There is no question in anyone's mind that he was bright as a dollar and going somewhere in life in a conspicuous fashion.

When he started his soon-to-be-great engineering and construction company in Paris, it was under the Eiffel name. Early on, the firm designed and built bridges and buildings all over Europe with great success. He worked on a variety of engineering challenges ranging from steam locomotives to design/build work on the locks for de Lesseps' Panama Canal fiasco.

Most notably, perhaps, his firm designed and built the structural frame for the Statue of Liberty. First, they built and completely erected it in Paris, then took it apart piece by piece, numbered the connections, shipped it to New York and then re-constructed it again on Liberty Island—right next to Ellis Island.

The original design of the Eiffel Tower was patented by three engineers: Koechlin, Nougier and Sauvestre. Gustave bought their patent, gave it his name and constructed the tower for the Exposition Universelle in 1889. This event celebrated the 100-year anniversary of the fall of the Bastille which launched of the French Revolution. In order to be awarded the commission to build the tower, Eiffel negotiated an unusual contract with the City of Paris. Roughly, he agreed to foot 80% of the construction cost in exchange for the subsequent 20 years of revenue produced from the attraction. At that point in time, the tower was supposed to be removed from the site. So, of course, he built a penthouse for himself at the very tip top of the spire. I mean, like, who wouldn't?

Now, did he invite Princes and Presidents and the likes of Thomas Edison, the world's most famous inventor, to come visit him at his penthouse in the tower? Well, of course he did. That's what real guys did in those days. And don't forget, Parisians, by and large, hated the iron and steel monstrosity violating their pastoral skyline. Edison loved it—and praised it generously.

In his retirement years, Gustave built wind tunnels to test airplane airfoils. This way, he translated to mathematical formulae, Bernoulli's principals of gas velocities affecting pressure. Remember? "Higher velocity creates lower pressure," which in turn, gives lift to an aircraft wing—no small feat to quantify into a calculus form. He also set up small weather stations to advance the science of meteorology. Eiffel, like Edison, knew few scientific or intellectual boundaries.

He died at his mansion in Paris while listening to Beethoven's 5th Symphony. Isn't that the piece with the famous dot-dot-dot-dash, the Morse Code for V (for Victory)?

Okay, kids, so much for history. Lecture's over. Just remember, "It's not just what you see, it's.........."

When we arrive at the tower, we have a short discussion about taking the elevator to "the top." Even though she is a pilot, any edge that has any sense of "precipice" will set off internal alarms. After some discussion, I agree with her—that, for our purposes, the "top" of the Eiffel Tower is going to be that big platform upon which the long skinny, antenna thing stands.

There is an elevator that may go to the very *tip-top*, but we will only go to the *"the top"* as *we* define it.

Even after having negotiated *our* top, Mitch is still not very comfortable. But she sticks it out. The wind is picking up and, as evening approaches, the temperature is easing down to the chilly range. Acrophobia or not, she agrees that the view of Paris with the Seine running through it is spectacular. We spend a half an hour just trying to assimilate the wonder of this city. Without question, Paris is a picture of the perfect blend of chaos and order. Finally, and to Mitch's relief, we take the elevator down and catch a taxi back to the hotel. Taxi fares seem to average about ten dollars a pop.

Dinner is at a small restaurant we found by chance three blocks from the hotel. It's on a narrow street, almost an alley.

**FROM THE FIRST PLATFORM LEVEL OF
THE EIFFEL TOWER (HIGH ENOUGH)**

The front door is glass with sheers behind it that make it hard to see inside. Next to the door is a small window just the size of their menu. Inside, however, it is bright and clean and attended by waiters in starched white shirts and bow ties. They hustle attentively, but not so much as to be annoying. There are twenty other costumers; the dining room is about half full. The atmosphere is family, fragrant, and friendly.

Mitch orders trout, and I have veal, and we each have a glass of house white. This is a comfortable place. If we stay longer in Paris, it may become *our place*.

Our simple and delicious meal is a classy way to finish a day. The walk back to the hotel is slow and easy. Lights out at 10:30.

DAY 4
PARIS

Last night offered a poor night's rest for both of us—must be the ole jet-lag hangover. As compensation, we are going to have an extra leisurely breakfast of coffee, assorted rolls, and fruit in the greenhouse.

The completely relaxed atmosphere here makes this a good time to plan an inventive next step. Even though we have hardly tasted Paris, for some reason we jump ahead to tomorrow. Almost out of the blue, we decide that in the morning, we will take the 187 mph bullet train to Barcelona. Other than the fact that Mitch has always wanted to go there, there is no particular reason for picking it. The front desk gives us directions to a train reservations office two blocks away. There, we buy two first-class tickets to Nimes, France. From there, we will catch a local train to Barcelona. From hotels.com on my cell phone, I select the Espania Hotel just off La Rambla, and I make reservations for $250/night.

With tomorrow's agenda now in the oven, we catch a taxi to the Basilica Sacre Coeur de Montmartre. The weather today is trying to be normal for March (i.e., chilly, drizzly and overcast). The taxi ride offers plenty of street scenes of alleys and side parks but, unfortunately, only takes about twenty-five minutes. It's a wonderful drive through the morning confusion of a town getting ready for a day's work.

The low overcast restricts visibility from The Mont to less than two miles. This adds to the feeling of exclusivity of this sacred place. Drizzle or not, the architecture of the basilica itself is still stunning. After a twenty-minute tour through the cathedral, we wander around the neighborhood on the hill and come across a small, brick chapel set back from the street behind some old trees. The simplicity of the design catches Mitch's fancy. Inside there is not a lick of gold anywhere. It's a strictly fundamental Christian/Catholic architecture. In its own humble-human way, it really is quite spiritual. It makes you want to finally sit down and not be wowed. Maybe the scarcity of glamor is something of a relief. For some reason, I feel more generous to their donations box than normal. And it has nothing to do with religion. Figure that one out.

Just around the corner from the Humble Church is a small city park filled with artists ready to paint or draw portraits of tourists. A canopy of fresh-budding trees shelters the whole block with green lace. The level of artistic accomplishment displayed on easels is surprisingly high, and some of the work is truly exceptional. However, we take a pass on the art and ride on the forty-five-degree funicular 150 feet down the hill into the old commercial part of town. The

MONTMARTRE

first order of business is to share a Haagen-Dazs ice-cream sundae at a local sweet shop that smells of aging milk and fresh chocolate. It's the perfect pick-me-up. We then catch a taxi back to our base of operations—the Notre-Dame.

In spite of the weather being chilly and drizzly, we make the unlikely decision to take the red, glass-covered, sightseeing-boat tour on the Seine. The loading dock for these excursions is not shown on our map, so we end up walking probably two miles up and down the riverbanks before we finally find their ticket office tucked up almost under a bridge. The search for this facility has taken us the entire distance that the boat will cover. But we buy two tickets anyway. Besides, the hike just earned us some serious sit-down time.

To get down to the boat dock, we have to descend a long set of stone stairs from street level. It then goes down farther through a tunnel to the riverbank. On the way, we encounter thirty folks in white robes, boots, flags, and banners that announced themselves as being *Cavalieri Templari Christiani*. I wonder if this was a sect that operated during the Crusades. I Googled them on my cellphone but could find nothing in English that helped in my identification. They sure looked content and peaceful on the steps. Their quiet manner suggested that something nice was going on.

We eventually get our tickets and weigh on board at twenty bucks each. The weather has become even a little chillier. But we're doing exactly what we set out to do (i.e., take a boat ride)! All but a few of the not-many passengers ride in the large enclosed cabin amidships. We sit up in the bow of the boat, in the drizzle like Templar Crusaders headed to free the Holy Land. The temperature is right on

THE CAVALIERI TEMPLARI CHRISTIANI

the cusp of cold and freezing-ass cold. As we cruise along, there is absolutely nothing to see that we didn't see closer-up and personal an hour ago. The chilly sprinkle that drove the other passengers inside affords us a splendid feeling of a private outing on the river. As exciting as this is, however, I assure you that we're not in the least bit disappointed when we finally get out of the rain and return to the shelter of our embarkation point.

It's about a mile and a half from the dock to the hotel, so we hoof it back through the Left Bank labyrinth of small, narrow streets. We use only guess, intuition and a rough sense of destination to find our way. If we're lucky, we'll get lost along the way and discover who knows what. The physical activity gets our circulation going again. This feels really good, and the gut navigation works out just fine. The reward is that we, once again, have an ample dinner at the Café Cassette. But this time I don't bother with a tip. I mean, how good can it get?

We've done a pretty good job of hitting the traditional highlights of Paris in the last two days. But we have missed Versailles. Our loose plan now is to return here a day or two early from wherever we end up and then catch the Sun King's Palace. We'll simply have to wait to see how all the rest of our time works out. There is a pedometer on my iPhone. It reads 6.2 miles today. Hmm. That's a Peachtree Road Race. All we were missing was sixty-thousand other runners and Fourth of July temperatures.

THE SEINE FROM A TOUR BOAT

DAY 5
Paris

Both of us wake up at 4:00 a.m. without the cell phone alarm going off. We're 90 percent packed and head down to an early breakfast at 7:15.

Mitch is in a big hurry. The Bullet Traain doesn't leave until 10:40, so what's the hurry? As we get to the dining room, she says she believes the train leaves at 8:40. She holds the tickets, but I bought them. I don't need to see them to know she's simply wrong. I have all this schedule stuff worked out in my head. So I'm just bumping along enjoying the morning. When I finally do get around to double-checking the departure time on the tickets, it turns out that she's right, and I've been gumming up the whole operation.

A guy can make a mistake once in a while, can't he?

To get things back on track, she hustles down to the front desk and quickly pays the hotel bill ($1,000) and asks the front desk to call us a taxi. I finish up the packing and bring down the bags and try to catch up. The train station is not far, and we make it there quickly—fifteen minutes—and with twenty-five minutes to spare, and tickets already in hand.

Mitch talks to an information booth clerk, and he says that our train is at track nineteen. We scurry over to nineteen, still in anticipation of being late. The train is still sitting there, and there are people running to get on board. So we hustle, too. I get there first and climb aboard. Mitch gets caught in the sliding doors of the car, and a couple of guys force the doors back open for her. It recycles, and she jumps in. The door closes. Man, that was close.

But we make it!

Since we have expensive first-class tickets we climb up the half-dozen steps into the upper-level observation deck. Actually, there doesn't seem to be as much distinction in the classes as I thought there would be. Hmm, must be the New France. But there is something else wrong. The train, which is clean, quiet, and nice in every respect, is not my idea of a bullet train. We're just chugging along like a Metro. Besides, the fancy electronic sign over the door says the next stop is Versailles. Versailles is in the suburbs of Paris, isn't it?

Almost immediately after we pull out of the Paris Station, we realize that we have gotten on the wrong train! This train, the one we rushed to catch, had not yet vacated track nineteen to make room for our real Barcelona bullet to pull into. We were a few minutes too early!

As strange as this sounds, we just sit here and sort of laugh. Well, it's not really a laugh. It's only a smile with raised eyebrows. We look at each other and, without words, say, "You know, it really doesn't make that much difference. Does it?"

We do a surprisingly good job of relaxing during the twenty minutes it takes to get to the Versailles terminal. There, we get off and, in no sense of hurry, walk over to the other platform, sit and wait ten minutes, and then get back on the next train headed back to Paris.

Now, I have to backtrack a little. The error we just made was clearly mine. Thinking I had caused us to be late, I overreacted and got to charging too hard. But what is important to note, is that this blunder didn't cast the least shadow on our moods. Maybe it even added to the adventure. Remember: we're just winging it, and serendipity is all part of the program. This event is further proof that we are finally separating from the rigid, orderly, disciplined procedures that over-govern our everyday lives. Besides, Mitch gets a star in her crown for not ever bringing up my error again—even subtly like we all do sometimes. Maybe she's starting a collection of silent stars. Who knows?

The train ride back to Paris is pleasant enough. We haul our two suitcases—no, *I* haul our two suitcases—through the terminal. Mitch, who is in charge of all things paper (tickets, reservations, etc.), finds the right guy in the complaint/problem-solving department of the railroad station. It turns out that he had lived in California for five years and says our problem is not a big one. Our discussion about tickets is friendly and easygoing. He tells us there are no more bullet trains today, but he books us on a direct one tomorrow morning for $325 each This is forty dollars each cheaper than today's ride. Plus, we don't have to change trains in Nimes. I cell phone the Espania in Barcelona, and they shift our reservation a day at no charge. I then call Hotel L'Abby,

PALACE OF VERSAILLES

and they welcome us back. We catch a quick taxi there, and now we're back in the comfort and security of Paris.

In all of the hustle this morning, we left without breakfast. Now, welcomed back home to L'Abby, we are invited to sit in the garden café for a late coffee, rolls, and marmalade snack. Once refueled and rested, we're ready to start another day. It's only midmorning.

PALACE OF VERSAILLES

At noon we walk the mile to our Notre-Dame Metro Station and catch the local train to Versailles. It's a scenic ride running right along the banks of the Seine. The train then bends south to the same station we used briefly earlier this morning to return to Paris. Then it's still about a mile hike through mostly residential blocks to the entrance of Louis the XIV's chateau. The queue that has already formed in the huge open plaza is enormous. The single file, three-hundred-foot-long line is folded back on itself three times. Yes, that is a nine-hundred-foot-long line; I'm guessing four hundred people. We take our place at the bitter end. Immediately in front of us, we meet a very nice couple from North Carolina who live on the coast just south of Myrtle Beach. Thus starts a nice two-hour friendship.

I did not write down his name, but he is a business developer for Sysco Industries. I guess that means salesman. He is on his second marriage and has two grown daughters. His wife works from home on a computer. Her mother's name is Ruth Elinore (their spelling). They don't have any kids, but her father is my age (mid-eighties) and also a Korean War veteran. He got an early discharge because of some eye problem. One of them has another cousin who had the same problem—early military termination because of vision problems. Interesting, huh? No. Of course not. It's dull as dishwater. But I include it here because this is what you talk about waiting in line for two hours.

We finally bid *au revoir* to our new friends. But those couple of hours together set a remarkable tone of trust and friendship. It is a valuable reminder of one of those precious little things in the human discourse.

Standing in line is exhausting. No two ways about it. But once we're in the chateau and rubbing elbows with all the *touristas maximus*, we're back into sure-enough real work. Actually, real work beats standing in lines by leagues.

Once inside the great halls, the design and execution of the Palace of Versailles is simply beyond my ability of expression. Every room, every molding, every chandelier, the floors, the walls, the ceilings, the gold and gilding are all extravagant expressions of the human fantasy. One can only be left emotionally exhausted at the scale of extravagance.

We leave at 4:45 and walk the mile back up to the train station and arrive in Paris at 5:30. This time we blow through the station like old but unperfumed Parisians.

Since Paris is a confusing network of streets and alleys, we sure could use a map. Unfortunately, we still don't have a good one. So we venture out, just guessing directions and, again, make no wrong turns. This is another good excuse to reward ourselves with one more repast at the Café Cassette. Mitch orders a club sandwich on toast, and I have brim ceviche (sixty-five dollar check). It ain't cheap here. We're back at L 'Abby at 7:00, tired, stuffed and happy. My phone reads 7.3 miles on the pedometer. This app does not record the standing hours in the lines of Versailles.

DAY 6

Paris to Barcelona

T oday will be our second shot for the Bullet to Barcelona.

A good night's sleep is any man's blessing. Thankfully, I had asked Siri to wake us at 8:00 a.m. Otherwise, I think we'd still be out cold. We both pack quickly and go down to the desk at 8:45. Mitch again generously picks up the hotel tab and once more asks the desk to call a taxi. We wolf down some coffee and a pastry, but not quickly enough. We miss our taxi. The second one arrives at 9:20. Anxieties come rumbling back. Of course it is rush hour now, and we need to get to the Lyon Train Terminal, which is halfway across town.

But not to worry. Paris rush hour must start after lunch or something. We breeze straight to the station and arrive at

9:45 for a 10:08 departure. This time we check for the correct track and give it a little time for any previously lingering train to depart. I think we're starting to get the hang of things.

The train looks to be a mile long. The aero-sloped nose and polished red fuselage reek of speed. We find car twelve, seats ninety-four and ninety-five on the upper level, and share the table with an Asian mother and her teenage son sitting opposite us. Shortly, we silently drift out of the station exactly on time, and I mean to the second.

The son is already playing thumb games with his cell phone. We haven't spoken a word to one another, but when the ticket-checker conductor comes by, their conversation is in English. Both of their accents are so strong I cannot understand the content of either end of the conversation. The son doesn't say a word.

At exactly 12:00, the mom gets up and goes downstairs somewhere and brings back two box lunches. The boy has thick, straight, black hair pulled back in a ponytail. There is another loose chunk that hangs down over one eye. He wears a very thin mustache and wispy chin whiskers. But there is no question that Mama is still in charge.

Mama looks to be more Mongolian than south Asian. Actually, she looks like a man until she smiles. Then her eyes light up, and she is clearly feminine—and actually an attractive mom.

Her husband, the boy's father, holds the rank of major and is a battalion commander in the Mongolian Arctic Border Patrol. His primary mission is to oversee security in the upper regions of Asia, east of the Siberian gulags and over toward Alaska. To his disappointment, the son is really not

BULLET-TRAIN TABLE MATES

a soldier-type like himself, but he's bright and has been accepted into the most highly regarded military school in China. He's an only child, and Mom is taking him on his *grand tour* before school starts in July. Then, off goes all the hair, and his cell phone is replaced with an AK-something.

Now how do I know all this? Easy. We all do it all the time. You just look at someone long enough when they are not looking back, and you figure it all out. We shared not a single word between us, and there was never any real eye contact. You just listen for vibes, and there they are. Let's call it ICT—imaginary commuter telepathy.

Now, telepathically charged, I look over at another couple sitting across the aisle, but one table further away. They are facing one another, in their seventies, nicely quaffed with whitish hair, clear complexions, and stylishly dressed. There is no question that they are French and a little blue-blooded. She has several dangly neckless chains and too many rings on her fingers. He wears a deep-purple silk scarf and a gold wristwatch. I'd tell you all about them except, unlike the battalion commander's son, most of their stuff is confidential and, quite frankly, some of it is really a little sordid. You see, she has this checkered past that goes way back to when…

Well, I've already said too much, so back to business.

The silent power of this train is amazing. There are no sensations of motors running or even of movement. At the very start of this journey, there was none of the excitement of old-fashioned jerking into motion. Remember the chain reactions of car-couplings clasping sequentially. As I said, on this train, the station simply begins to slide silently away; you gradually fade into another world like partial anesthesia.

As we pick up a head of steam (or electro-magnetic impulses), the engineering genius becomes even more impressive. I text a message back home to the kids, "It is so quiet and butter-smooth in here that it feels like we're stationary while a panoramic view of rural France flows silently by on back-lit movie screens built into the wall."

Yesterday I was awed by the extraordinary architectural accomplishments of Versailles. The day before, it was the Louvre. Today it is a silent, horizontal rocket ship that left on time, *to the second*, and traveled back in space-time. And it's all done by the French.

Man! What a culture!

Northern France, as it whisks by, is fertile farmland with the spring planting just getting underway. Middle France changes from large, groomed fields to smaller acreage of more irregular patches of agriculture mixed with cows. As we approach the Pyrenees Mountains, the rural architecture changes from stone and masonry to stucco and tile roofs. And now we're paralleling the coast line of the Mediterranean Sea. We're whizzing by a variety of contemporary residential developments mixed with old coastal architectural remembrances. We should be in Barcelona in an hour. Mitch just won a beer by being the first to see the sea. The *"first to see* (a destination) *gets a beer"* is an old game we have played since we first started dating. Unapologetically, she interrupted the writing of this narrative to point this out. And she doesn't drink beer!

At 2:00 p.m. we have sandwiches and Cokes from a vender coming down the center aisle. The lunch offerings are reminiscent of convenience market fast food. But it really is convenient, and we really are hungry. *C'est la vie!*

As we approach the Barcelona terminal, the train gradually slows and eases silently into the station. Carrying two suitcases down the multiple levels of the railroad car turns out to be a fairly gymnastic exercise for this old goat. But we bumble through it and emerge into the plaza.

FRANCE @ 200KPH

The *green light* taxis are all waiting off in a parking area to the right. We load in the first one in line and tell the driver, "La Hotel Espania, por favor." As I mentioned, I found this place on my cell phone a couple of nights ago and made reservations. It is located midway between the Columbus statue down here at the harbor's edge and the large Catalonia Park up the hill. La Rambla is about a mile-long concourse that connects these two landmarks with a huge pedestrian boulevard loaded with trees and street venders and cafes from one end to the other. Vehicular traffic is relegated to narrow service roads on either side. In a way, it's the Champs-Élysées of Barcelona, but much less grand in size and much more human in scale.

An important distinction between the two is that the Champs is a grand vehicular boulevard with pedestrian areas on either side. La Rambla is the reverse. It is a grand pedestrian boulevard with vehicular circulation set off to the sides.

The Espania Hotel is hidden a block down a cramped alleyway perpendicular to La Rambla. The buildings lining the alley are an interesting mix of traditional and modern architecture, but they all seem to blend agreeably with one another.

We check in, and our room turns out to be hardly larger than the queen-sized bed. But the interior design is dazzling. The lighting arrangement is commercial/theatrical with a full luminous wall and several high-intensity spots in the floor shining up to the ceiling. In terms of pizazz, it is exceptional. In terms of usefulness, it's a little iffy, especially in the bathroom. Recessed high-intensity ceiling can-lights above the mirror create hollow-eyed gargoyles in the reflection. They need to be moved a foot closer to the mirror. I look like Boris Karloff, if you remember him. Other than that, the glitz is definitely fun.

After our six hours on the train, no matter how smooth it was, we're ready to stretch our legs. We head straight to the Mediterranean Sea: downhill, just on the other side of the monumental Columbus statue.

The first order of business is dinner. On one of the docks is a tourist-swanky seafood place. The view of the harbor is great, the service and food are both okay, and the cost is fair. But that's about it. No complaints. Gets the job done.

After dinner, we walk back along the docks and marvel at the pleasure boats and yachts. The rich and famous who visit here on their yachts are off the scale in luxury.

All the main streets here in town are a bustling motor scooter arena. We later learn that Barcelona has the highest per capita ratio of motorbikes to people in Europe. For some reason, they seem to fit better here than Paris. It must be that scale thing again.

What a very nice day it has been.

COLUMBUS STATUE AT SUNSET

DAY 7

Barcelona

We're up at eight o'clock and catch a taxi to run us up to the Sagrada Familia basilica, Gaudi's almost finished cathedral masterpiece. Morning tours are already booked up, so we buy tickets for 1:00 p.m. This is good. It gives us time to prowl around the city a little bit.

First, we walk a mile over to the Casa Mila, Gaudi's other incredible *tour de force*. Most of the juicy architectural stuff here is either on the roof, in the attic, or on the top floor. The six-story climb up a set of thirty-inch-narrow stairs is tough. As mentioned at the Eiffel Tower, Mitch is wary of heights. So I tour around the roof alone while she sits in the doorway of the access stair. We are both thoroughly absorbed by the genius of design of this whole place. Gaudi was not only a big-idea architect, blazing the southern front of Europe for the *art nouveau* movement, and then going on in the early twentieth century, but also he designed down to the finger pulls on kitchen cabinets. We make it a point to pick up little Gaudi gifts for architect friends in the gift store. Everything here carries the magic of his spirit.

And, yes, I bought a finger pull for my daughter-in-law, Sara. She is not only an architect, a landscape architect, but also an Iberian princess as well. The small "p" in princess is because her royal position is recognized only by my son and immediate family. Few are better informed to appreciate Gaudi's genius better than she.

After doing our architectural duties, we catch a taxi back to the Sagrada Familia where we enjoy a light lunch in a one-table corner deli. This place is smaller than our average-sized kitchen at home. For some reason, the Coca Cola we split is the most refreshing one ever served anywhere!

THE ROOF OF CASA MILA

After lunch, we hook up with our tour leader at the front entrance of the cathedral and start the circuit. As you can see from the pictures, this architecture is simply beyond my ability to describe.

Let me introduce you to the Architect.

Yesterday, as we were riding the "bullet" from Paris to Barcelona, I dutifully noted changes in geological composition and the regional architecture zipping by. Other than the topography of the Pyrenees Mountains, the variations were subtle. What I could *not* see out the window at 187 MPH, were the deeply embedded cultural differences. Defining these qualities takes an eye more experienced and practiced than mine. But I know whose I'd like to use—Antoni Gaudi. This was a man who expressed cultural ideologies more elegantly than any one I know of. It is deeply encoded in all of his work.

THE APSE OF THE SAGRADA FAMILIA

Sorry class. It's lecture time again. But, before we start, another quick aside.

If Eiffel was an engineering genius with an incredible eye for the aesthetic, then Gaudi was an aesthetic-genius with an incredible eye for engineering. Visionaries both? Yes. But they never saw the art-form of architecture from the same perspective.

Antoni was born here in Catalonia in June, 1852, twenty years after Eiffel was born. He died in 1926, three years after Gustave's death. As contemporaries, each in his own way, poured volatile fuel into the Industrial Revolution sweeping through the Western World. But, as I said, their approaches to the use of technology in architecture were as different as the human imagination can muster.

Where Eiffel stepped up and grabbed technology by the horns and proudly showed the world what it was all about, Gaudi never wavered in his conviction that "art and emotion" were the spiritual guidon bearers for cultural expression. To him, technology was a means, not an end.

At the Barcelona Higher School of Architecture, he studied French, history, philosophy, *and aesthetics.* Although academically adequate, his early passion for arts and his natural gift for crafts expressed itself more vividly. Engineering-wise, his intuitive understanding of the use of the catenary arch as a natural solution for structural spans was revolutionary. Catenary arch, you ask?

Envision, if you will, you are holding the two ends of a string of pearls. The curvature of the pearls is a natural distribution of forces. Invert it, and you have the St Louis Arch—the iconic catenary arch! The Romans used their perfectly rounded Roman Arches and the Gothics their pointy Ogee Arches. Gaudi mastered the *inverted string of pearls*. If you Google *catenary arch*, then hit *images*, you'll get an eye-full of Gaudi.

As you would expect, Gaudi's drawing talents were excellent. But, even in his pinnacle years as an architect, he minimized the use of this skill to almost nil. To communicate with his clients and craftsmen, he built models or did hands-on crafting. Rather than using his glorious renderings, he hand-sculpted his architecture.

On a personal level, unlike most high-achievers in any field of endeavor, he remained reserved and, perhaps, contemplative. Even as a young architect, he adopted strict vegetarian rules and on several occasions undertook lengthy and severe fasts: some even life-threatening. On the other hand, his Faith in his Church offered him immeasurable comfort. His religious commitment was so conspicuous that he earned the nickname, *God's Architect*.

So, when I walk through one of his pieces of architecture, do I feel the same spiritualism Gaudi worked so hard to ingrain into it? Probably not. But then, I'm just a pedestrian cynic from the old school.

However, in the Sacrada Familia, I do feel lots of *something* going on inside me. It's more like awe and wonder. It's like my brain waves seep out and want to go where Gaudi's brain once explored, to see what he saw, to share his creativity just a little bit. But whatever that *something* is, to this old goat, his work comes as close to *spiritual* as anything this side of holding your own baby at childbirth.

His work has no equal. Nothing even comes close.

Many parts of Gaudi's life-story were both resplendent and fanciful. Other parts reserved and maybe even dark. He never married. Hence he was unencumbered with all those years of marital bliss that so many lesser architects struggle with. The sum-total of his extraordinary life was too rich a story to even begin to recount here. Suffice it to say that his glory years were enchanting and fulfilling to the extreme. The lean ones bordered on the edges of tragedy.

At seventy-seven years old, while walking to his daily prayer and confessions at the St Felip Neri church in Barcelona, he was hit by a tram. As was his style in his later years, he was shabbily dressed and unkempt in appearance. He carried neither credentials nor money. The officials at the scene of the accident thought the victim to be a down-and-out fellow and directed that he be taken to the pauper's ward in the hospital. There he died several days later. When his identity was finally discovered, he was buried in a sacred crypt in the catacombs of his Basilica Sagrada Familia.

It occurs to me that this life could well be a Parable in the Book he so fully revered. I have to believe that in his final hours, he saw his life that way too.

His last words were, "Amen, my God, my God."

These two calls to God ring a little of his Savior's last words.

When the tour is over, we take a Red Line open-air bus tour and enjoy just riding around in the sunshine. As in the Paris tour busses, it has jacks for earplugs to point out the city sights. Along the way, we drive right by Gaudi's city park project. We'll come back to see this later when we have more time. The bus keeps weaving about until we come

SAGRADA FAMILIA

to the old Gothic area of town. This district feels seriously medieval. Eventually we walk by the Colon Hotel, where my friend Larry Thorpe and I stayed with our sons seven or eight years ago. Larry is the godfather of our three children, and I the godfather of his son, Benjamin. I tell Mitch the boys-being-boys on La Rambla story for the umpteenth time (i.e., Ben-got-rolled/Richard-disappeared). She endures it patiently—which might mean she's not listening anymore.

BARCELONA

We walk back through blocks of narrow streets to our hotel and get the name and location of a travel agency that might help us with a crazy notion—to go from Barcelona to Rome by ship! I've been on my cell phone trying to Google such a voyage. All of the advertisements I find seem to have contradictions of utility versus comfort. The only ships I can locate to make the trip are ferry boats, and they only have single staterooms with four bunks each; and they are either for men or women only.

To get better advice, we walk up to a travel agency at Catalonia Park. Unfortunately, the young lady we meet claims to know almost nothing about sea travels. But she does know all the other travel tricks. Nonetheless, she calls up a ferry line and talks with them a few minutes. She covers the phone and says that it sounds all right to her.

She then asks, "Shall I do it?" I nod and she asks me, "Inside or outside stateroom?"

I say, "Inside." She books us on a ferryboat and writes down the dock address on a folder and hands it to me. I still have an image of ferryboat/tramp steamer. However, the fare is fifty dollars each. Four fares cost $200. So I book *four* fares and this gives us our own stateroom for whatever gender we want to call ourselves. And we have some elbow room to boot.

This is a big step in taking some uncertainty out of the equation. The agent also books us a hotel in Civitavecchia, the port city for Rome. We figure what the heck. If the trip is awful, it *will* eventually end, and we'll have a nice hotel in Italy to get over it.

Still, this is risky stuff. I glance over at Mitch for the expected sign of disapproval or, at least, apprehension. There is neither. And I mean absolutely no opinions expressed or implied.

Since cookies and milk at bedtime is my only bad habit, on the way back to the hotel, we stop for a takeout snack at a tiny tobacco shop. We have to settle for vanilla cookies and a whole liter of Coke.

Directly across the street from the little store is a side door to the opera house that fronts around the corner on La Rambla. It's 7:50 p.m., and we're dog tired. A billboard next to the side door shows that *Rigoletto* is playing tonight. It starts at eight. I look at Mitch, and she shrugs. Without a word of discussion, I then trot around the corner to the ticket booth and purchase two tickets on the fourth balcony. We're quickly seated in this elegant opera hall with three minutes to curtain time. We're also seriously underdressed—at least I am. I'm wearing jeans, a tweedy jacket and an open-necked flannel shirt. Mitch looks better. She has on black slacks and a buff-colored woolen jacket of matronly style. The other attendees to this event are in jewelry and dinner jackets. I also have the jumbo-sized, plastic bottle of Coke in one jacket pocket and big bag of cookies stuffed in the other.

The first act of the opera is a full hour of intense musical drama of anguish and emotion. Giuseppe Verdi is in full song swinging his mighty musical sword. The stage set is no more than a set of red stairs without railings rising fifteen feet above the stage. All action takes place either on the stairs, behind them, or to each side. The power of brutal visual simplicity played against the complexity of Verdi's magical splendor is successful beyond one's imagination. The projection of the orchestra is full and strong and the acoustics clear and balanced. The pianissimos are as stunning as the crescendos.

The first act is one hour long, and the intermission is scheduled for forty minutes. But we are physically *burnt toast*. When we get up to walk around a bit, we find ourselves slowly inching to the front door—dreamily contented. For us, this has been the perfect one-hour performance.

And too much of even a good thing is still too much. Our cultural sponge is saturated.

Gaudi all day and Verdi all night will spin anybody's compass.

Thus endeth another day. By the way, the tickets for the opera were $175 each—for us a very expensive impulse item. But, in the end, it turned out to be an investment of

BARCELONA

RIGOLETTO

incalculable satisfaction. It was simply the right thing at the right time.

The hotel is on the same block as the opera house, except it's on a side street, not on La Rambla. Either way, the front entrance looks magnitudes better at night than during the day. Having light glowing out on the rather darkish, narrow street is pretty classy. We are moths seeking a flame.

As we walk into the front lobby, we are so tired that we almost hold hands like old folks. But we don't. Either we are not yet that old, or we are not yet that tired. Let's hope it's both.

DAY 8

Barcelona

After a great night's sleep, we're up and out the Espania door at 8:30 a.m. to commence the requisite morning stroll up the big, lineal tourist magnet—La Rambla. As I said, vehicular traffic is restricted to two, two-lane drives on either side of a generous pedestrian way down the middle. This is where all of the ice-cream venders, magazine/postcard booths, children's impulse toy sales, umbrella stands, and food carryout businesses are conducting mercantile enterprises. We walk on through the transient commerce going on, up the hill to the Catalonia Park end of the boulevard to revisit yesterday's travel agency.

Last night, I emailed Damon. I have been his Big Brother since he was nine years old, nearly fifty years ago. He's now an architect making his mark in New York City. His son, Holden, is a junior at Tulane in a study-abroad program in Venice. In response to my email, I get Holden's email address. I then emailed Holden and set up a date for Nancy and me to visit him in V-town next week. This requires us to exchange a little bit of serendipity for some old-fashioned planning. But I gotta admit something here. I'm about ready.

Again, we meet the same travel agent who, yesterday, booked our tramp/ferry boat ride to Italy. Airline reservations are second nature to her. So in three minutes flat, she has us booked on an Air France flight from Venice to Paris after our visit with Holden. It looks like that will close the European loop.

Finally, with our long-range planning taken care of, we walk back down La Rambla for breakfast at a sidewalk café. Mitch orders a great-looking, great-smelling mushroom omelet, and I have an ordinary ham and cheese on white sandwich bread. I don't know what I was thinking.

We watch the endless stream of tourists saunter by for a while, then it's back to the Espania to check out.

LA RAMBLA

Our ship doesn't leave until 10:00 p.m. tonight. This gives us plenty of time to head back up La Rambla to Catalonia Park, the origin of all tour-bus itineraries. We again catch an upper-deck seat on a tour bus that goes all over the seashore (south) side of town and then up Montjuïc. On the way up the steep hill, through the trees, we catch a glimpse of Mies van der Rohe's Barcelona Pavilion.

In terms of architectural philosophy, or design execution, Mies is the polar opposite to Gaudi. Mies is "form follows function." Gaudi is "function (and everything else) succumbs to form." Of course, these are gross oversimplifications. But still, they are both geniuses in the execution of their individual philosophy.

To get down to the Barcelona Pavilion, we have to continue up on past it to the museum parking lot perched on the very top of the mountain (really just a healthy hill). Then we get off the bus and walk back down a long series of stairs and terraces to get to the pavilion. The descent is on a rather luxurious grand stairway with an engaging view of the city. We pay the $2.50 entrance fee and walk up and into the masterpiece of iconic architecture. In my opinion, the magical *power of simplicity* is nowhere better expressed more clearly *in any art form* than in this one piece of architecture. The building was finished in 1929, six years before I was born. In terms of architectural design, it is still light years ahead of anything now being produced.

With our architectural appreciation tank now topped off, we hike back up the long stairs to the parking plazas to catch the bus back to Catalonia Park. From there we will take another open-air bus to cover the other side of the city.

THOUGHTFUL? OR JUST POOPED OUT?

Incidentally, my pitch to Mitch to take the two-mile cable car ride from the top of Montjuïc to downtown Barcelona falls on deaf ears. No surprise there.

Once we're back to Catalonia Plaza, we catch the Blue Line bus that covers the other (north) half of Barcelona. Of course, this time we stop for several hours at Guell Park, Gaudi's landscape/planning *magnum opus*.

With enthusiasm from only one of us, we start the long climb to the very top of the forested park. The other one of us says, "Well if you have to climb to the very top of everything, just go right ahead. Personally, I don't have to." When the one who has to climb to the top gets there, it is only a few minutes later that the one who doesn't have to also arrives there. The second one almost smiles. The story of Sir Edmund Hillary and "because it's there" falls on the same ears that declined the cable car ride. Nonetheless, we take some great selfies from the top. That's Montjuïc in the background and the Mediterranean Sea on the horizon.

The view down on the city is enchanting. The horizon of the Mediterranean frames the backdrop. We skylark (old army term for just spooking around, not doing nothing) and rest for half an hour, and then work our way back down through a fantasy of walls, tiles, small buildings with wonderful chimneys, and intimate plazas. Gaudi is everywhere.

It's a mile walk to find a taxi back to La Rambla. Once there, we stop to eat at a large and lively, open-air *mercado*. The vender's arcades have all nature of food stuffs and eateries distributed over a hundred stalls. Sitting at a lunch counter with working-class locals, Mitch and I share shrimp kabobs, salad, and asparagus. I'm sure there must be other tourists

THE TOP OF GUELL PARK

MERCADO IN BARCELONA

here, but it feels absolutely authentic. I mean, everybody's gabbing in a foreign tongue, aren't they?

It's finally time to hail a taxi to take us to the shipping docks. The cab weaves around shipping containers and piled-up freight and then right up to a fancy cruise liner. I mean, it is beautiful! It's a clean, modern, sleek full-blown ship. It looks to be seven hundred feet long, maybe more. I count ten decks above the water line. The what-we-used-to-call smokestack is raked and the superstructure sloped aerodynamically aft. I pull her up on the internet, and she's only ten years old. We smile in disbelief. The stars just aligned.

As it turns out, however, the ship really is also a traveling mega-ferry. First, hundreds of cars are driven on board, followed by what I counted to be eighty to one-hundred full-blown, eighteen-wheel tractor trailers. These are backed directly into the stern of the ship for easy unloading.

Now all this starts to make some sense. We foot-passengers are strictly ancillary income. The main source of revenue appears to be the cars and tractor trailers taking a short cut between central Italy and Spain and back. I just "Google Earthed" the road path between Barcelona and Rome, and it's about eight hundred miles—about three hundred miles longer than the sea route. And the sea route has zero stop signs.

Around midnight, from the tenth-deck lobby, we watch a steady stream of truck drivers coming up the stairs and elevators to where the game room, bar, casino, health room, dining room, and cafeterias are all located. Let the party begin!

After a quick look around on the seventh deck, we find our little stateroom deep in the bowels of the ship. It is very compact, with two single beds on the deck and two fold-up bunkbeds hinged to the walls. There, we collapse.

What a day!

A TRAMP STEAMER TO ROME?

Ad Lib

THE GAME ROOM

THE MAIN LOUNGE

DEPARTING BARCELONA HARBOR AT MIDNIGHT

DAY 9

The Mediterranean Sea

It's 6:30 a.m. The stateroom doesn't have a porthole, but I think we are at sea. When I thought this ship was a tramp steamer, my idea in picking an interior stateroom was that it wouldn't have a rusty, leaking porthole. Also, the area closest to the roll axis will have the least seasick movement in weather. But the weather last night was a complete meteorological non-event. I bet this ship even has gyroscopic roll stabilization.

We each had only a fair night's rest in our stateroom for four. *Rest* is the key word here. Sleep was nominal. The ship has almost no roll or pitch. It's solid as a rock. The engines don't throb or pound. It vibrates a little, but not to an annoying degree. Actually, in a way, the cadence is kind of soothing. The poor sleep probably came from the lack of

SUN DECK ON THE "FERRY BOAT"

SARDINIA OFF THE STARBOARD RAIL

windows and spatial uncertainty. A little touch of claustrophobia may enter into the formula.

The head in our stateroom (bunkroom, actually) is about three feet square with the lavatory-counter cut in a way to provide for the door swing. We're talking seriously tiny. I take a shower and flood the floor. This turns out to be the only shower drain. The big mirror over the sink helps a little to reduce the feeling of compression.

Right now, I'm sitting on my bunk waiting for Mitch to finish doing whatever always takes so much time for women to do in the head. (That's a nautical bathroom—not what's between their ears.)

Ahh. Finally!

She just finished.

CORSICA OFF THE PORT RAIL

Now we can go eat and see what the Mediterranean Sea looks like. I'm itching to explore, but we need to stick together for a while. This is like calibrating a GPS before a flight.

This ship is truly amazing. The interior design is pure modern glitz. The ceilings are mirrored. There are plenty of chrome railings and lots of modern furniture. The big spaces are generous and tatty plush; the carpet is highly designed patterns of flourishes and swirls. I think this is called *era design*.

Breakfast is in the cafeteria and exactly what you'd expect: scrambled eggs, bacon, toast, cereal, coffee, and milk. Again, no complaints. Breakfast is eleven dollars each, and it does the job in traditional cafeteria fashion. The rest of the morning is spent prowling, looking at the Mediterranean, and generally just wasting time.

I try to go down to the engine room to look around but get caught on a parking deck by a ship's officer (or lackey). My curiosity is not worth the hassle, so I return to the commercial level. This cruising duty is quite different from pounding sidewalks as we've been doing for the last week.

At 1:30, we order sandwiches in the cafeteria. Two hours later, the ship passes between the islands of Corsica and Sardinia.

Each island is only about two or three miles away. Both are compellingly mysterious. The weather holds flawless. The sea is without a whitecap, and there are just enough sea gulls to hold your attention forever. Since there are too few lounge chairs on deck for everyone, we spend much of the afternoon working in one of the big-windowed indoor lounges.

I think most would agree this experience at sea simply could not be planned ahead of time in Atlanta.

Mitch spends most of the day on her edits of *Roll the Pole*. This is a book I'm working on about flying a small airplane to the magnetic north pole. I put in a few hours on this journal. We are like a couple of kids trying to get our homework done before we get to go to the movies.

The docking event is scheduled for 7:30 this evening—right about sunset.

It's a classic evening, with the sun settling on the western horizon as we ease gently into the port of Civitavecchia, Italy. The ship uses no tugboats. It is self-docking. By leaning over the railing and watching the prop wash, it appears that the

ANOTHER CRUISE LINER AT CIVITAVECCHIA, ITALY

propellers are steerable to at least ninety degrees. They are located both fore and aft in the hull. She actually moves in sideways up to the dock. This is absolutely amazing technology and seamanship.

Almost everyone on board has a car or truck in the hold. So after we disembark, the couple dozen of us pedestrians have to catch a harbor bus that takes us to the front gate of the port facility. There is no tourist-welcoming terminal here. There are no impulse venders, restaurants, or doodad shops. This is a fenced-in government compound. Taxi cabs are not even allowed inside.

At the facility front gate, we walk out past two armed guards then continue the hike to our hotel. It's not far, probably less than a half mile along the grand boulevard. The night is very dark and beautiful, and smells of the sea. The broad promenade along the boulevard is well lit and friendly. Somehow Civitavecchia feels more industrial than like a tourist destination.

We arrive at the Rose of the Mediterranean Hotel. It's on the grand boulevard, but is, at best, not more than a two-star operation. There is only one gentleman operating the front desk. The hotel feels spookily wanting of other guests. We have a second-floor room with a fourteen-foot-high ceiling and a balcony overlooking the grand boulevard. This room is taken straight out of the nineteenth century. The windows start at the floor and go ten feet high, and the mosaic-tiled bathroom is big enough for a slumber party.

These reservations were made by the travel agent in Barcelona. I wonder if hotels.com might have given us a

The Mediterranean Sea

little better image of what is offered. But we're fine here. We're just hungry.

After we dump our suitcases in the room, we head down the main boulevard in search for a place to eat. Two blocks away, we come up on a friendly, family-type restaurant. It's modern Italianesque in style with white, square tile up to the high ceiling of stamped metal panels, and Mediterranean pictures on the walls. Rich kitchen smells do their share of marketing.

Holding court with all the patrons—except us—is a happy, local guy with his pocket-sized dog who seems equally tipsy. They sort of dance around talking to everybody. To us, he (and maybe both) just smile.

A colorful, glossy photograph of a collection of mouth-watering seafood in a giant bowl graces the cover of their menu. I'm starved, so I just point to it and say, "How about this." It looks impressively large.

But upon delivery, it is the biggest meal I have ever had placed before me—anywhere—easily enough food for six stevedores. The waitress, who speaks no English, puts a bib on both Nancy and me. I would name all the variety of seafood, except it's easier to just say "everything available in the Mediterranean Sea except Homer's serpents."

The meal is exceptionally delicious. Mitch helps me out, but only to a *ladies' limit*. I don't know if sopping up the leftover juices with fresh Italian bread is bad manners or not. But nobody looked offended.

In looking back at this, I think I figured it out. Apparently there wasn't enough communication between any of us for the waitress to say, "The picture on the cover of the menu is for communication of our variety of seafood only. Please select that which you wish to eat." I may have been the first patron who ever ordered the cover with all options. But who knows. Maybe I inadvertently just qualified for membership into the Royal Order of Esteemed Mediterranean Food Gluttons. More likely, however, the rapacious meal was just another one of those harmless things that enhance a greater experience. For sure, I'll never forget it, and that's what counts. As I say, the quality of the food was first-rate.

We turn in at 10:00 p.m., with one of us way too overstuffed.

DAY 10

Civitavecchia— Rome

We're up and going at 8:00 a.m. This is the beginning of another one of those almost indescribably perfect days—blue skies, light breeze, and about 65°F. My breakfast at the hotel is undercooked bacon and fried eggs. Mitch has cereal and tea. There are only four other people in the dining room, all women. The full seating will hold about fifty. The one waitress is quiet and thoughtful. I wonder if the seated women are staff.

We check out at the front desk with the same guy who was there late last night and walk the quarter mile to the station to catch the train to Roma Terminal. The train is a local, so we get to see a lot of the industrial-scape along the way. Judging from the massive piles of equipment and containers, there must be plenty of economic enterprise going on in the neighborhood.

Finally arriving in Rome, and after getting a little lost in their station, we weave our way to a secondary side-exit door to a quiet street. Since we have not booked a hotel, it's probably time to start giving some attention to that issue.

The first hotel we stop at is very nice, but it is also full. The gentleman at the desk says there is some big "thing" going on in town and that most hotels will also be full. Perfect! A little challenge is what we're looking for. Luggage still in hand, we start walking in the direction of the Colosseum. On the way we stop at an inexpensive-looking hotel. They, too, are full. Perhaps *perfect* was a little premature.

Playing with happenstance can be fun. But it's looking more and more like it's time to start getting serious about lodging. As we're working our way west toward the old Roman ruins, we walk past a Qatar Airlines office. They have posters of airplanes in their window, and Mitch thinks it's a travel agency. There are three trim and nattily dressed Middle Eastern guys and an attractive, dark-eyed young woman running the small office. On the walls are dozens of colorful posters of Middle Eastern cities. Mitch talks to the woman who carefully and politely explains that they are not a travel agency. I don't think this makes much of an impression because Ms. America just keeps on talking.

Boy, do I know that feeling!

The young lady then says there is an Airbnb just next door, but you have to go around to the other side of the block and find a certain door, then take a small, secret elevator up to the third floor and talk to Kristine. All this is a little complicated, so the young lady says she will go with us and help work it out. She then walks with us around the block and introduces us to Kristine. The Qatar woman is an accommodating and gracious gem from the old school. I *will* fly Qatar, if I get a chance.

Kristine is a perky twenty-year-old ball of energy with a sing-song voice that is almost shrill. She chirps rather than talks. But all of her chirping is positive and friendly. Our room is located back around the corner by the Qatar Airline office. Following Kristine, we walk around the block again and she opens a wrought iron gate to a small courtyard. Mitch and I squeeze in a tiny wire-grilled elevator cab that goes up and down the center of the square, open stairwell. Kristine flutters up the steps and beats us to the third floor.

Once off the elevator, we go through a heavily locked corridor door, down another darkish hall, and with a card key, she electronically opens the door to a room. It is small, neat, clean and nicely lit. The sill for the one window is four feet high, but that's fine. We can see other building roofs and lots of blue sky. And it does have its own bathroom! It's not as nice as the hotel in Barcelona—but it's everything we need. It is clearly better than the four-man stateroom on the ship. We're more than satisfied with the arrangement. The only glitch is that we can have the room for only one night.

It would be nice to stay here a couple of days. We take it anyway and dump our bags. The cost is sixty-five dollars per night.

Now it's time to go to town!

We elevator down to the main street and walk through a beautifully wooded city park with lots of Roman ruins and a scattering of either urban pioneers or old-fashioned derelicts all scattered about in recumbent positions. Then, way ahead, we spot the east elevation of the great Colosseum. I give Mitch my lecture on the differences in Greek and Roman architecture. She's heard it all before but doesn't complain. She nods once, so I'm pretty sure that she listened to at least some of it.

At the Colosseum, we get in the end of the forty-five-minute ticket line for our self-tour of the structure. The building is monumental, tragic, complex, and artistic and everything else grand to the extreme. But after only an hour and a half, we're ready to move on. For some reason, we're both having a little trouble maintaining a working level of energy.

The next destination is the Pantheon. Halfway there, still about a half mile away, we stop at the memorial to Vittorio Emanuele II. This thing is inconceivably colossal. The huge cast statues of warriors on horses on the top of a brilliant white marble temple-form is staggering in scale and overwhelming in grandeur. Power, grace, and elegance all come to mind. Heroic; that's the word I'm looking for.

As we work our way further downtown, we make another stop at a nice hotel, and this time find a room and make reservations for the next two nights. It's a fairly small place but upscale and costs $220 per night. We already wish we could have stayed at the Bnb. Our opinion is not about the difference in cost. I think it's about the proximity to culture. Besides, Kristine seriously *out personalities* this otherwise very nice gentleman working the desk here.

Mitch just smiled. She shares this opinion.

THE COLOSSEUM

THE COLOSSEUM

MEMORIAL TO VITTORIO EMANUELE II

THE FORUM

It takes an hour for us to get to the Pantheon. The line is twenty minutes long. The interior is fairly full with tourists, but the rand space under the oculus is not uncomfortably packed. Rather than waiting for a tour, we put three dollars in a machine and listen on headsets to twenty minutes of recorded history. Currently the formerly polytheistic Pantheon is part of the Catholic Church and is now in operation as a Christian basilica. Sorry about that, Jupiter. But you had your day.

The scale, simplicity, and spiritual power of the rotunda is magnificent, but that is about all there is to see/feel here. I hate to hear myself say that, but the competition for grandeur here in Rome simply raises the bar so high that it dulls the senses to everyday dazzling wonderment.

Next, we weave our way over to the Trevi Fountain. It's an easy twenty-minute walk through wagon-width Roman streets, often too narrow for cars. The area in front of the fountain is packed with tourists. We do the obligatory picture-taking and then start our forty-five-minute walk back to the Bnb.

THE PANTHEON

For dinner, we find a nice, almost-upscale restaurant just around the corner of our hotel. Mitch orders a good-looking seafood spread, and I, too, have a fish dinner, but not anything like the big one in Civitavecchia. On the way back to the Bnb, we stop for cookies and orange juice for a bedtime snack. The store doesn't carry milk. What is it with milk and Europeans?

DAY 11
Rome

First thing this morning, we check out of our Bnb. There's a little uncertainty about where to leave the keys to the gate and door, so I leave that up to Mitch to figure out. My job is to just carry luggage. She works something out with some guy carrying out the trash. I never do completely figure that one out.

Bags in hand, we flag down a taxi to take us across town to our almost-classy hotel (relative to the Bnb). Because of military barricades, the cab has to drop us off three blocks from our destination. The whole area is cordoned off for a European Economic Summit. Apparently this is the "thing" that is going on in town. We can get only as close as the yellow plastic ribbons that are almost a city block between us and the hotel.

Without hesitation, Mitch walks over to the closest soldier and, like Hannibal before her, takes on the whole Italian army. But, of course she prevails. We are assigned an officer to escort us past the ribbons to the hotel. We check in at the desk and leave our bags and come back out to just past the cordoned off area. Here we enjoy a very satisfying light breakfast at a small but carefully groomed and landscaped sidewalk café. One could get used to this level of endulgence.

Our next junket is the biggie: to walk across town to St. Peter's Basilica in the Vatican. The route goes along the Forum. This is an extraordinary half mile of sunken ruins from ancient Rome in its heyday. We have to stop at every structure, big and small, and take lots of pictures. After an hour of trolling through this city's not quite lost past, we cut cross the Tiber River and approach St. Peter's. As we get close to the grand piazza, we're respectfully approached by a trim and attractive young woman who represents a tour company that will arrange for our general admission ticket in only twenty minutes. This sounds good to us.

We go to their offices, and it costs sixty-five dollars each, and the twenty-minute wait then turns into an hour and a half. At least we get to mill around as opposed to standing in line. The timing offer was a come-on, but the subsequent history tour is pretty good. While our group is waiting to get into the basilica, some guy comes around passing out free tickets left and right to everyone in sight. They look like free promotional movie tickets to me. Rather than throwing them away, I give mine to Mitch and comment on the movie aspect of it.

When it is time to enter the basilica, Mitch cannot find the little entry tickets we're supposed to have, to put in the turnstile. Somewhat abruptly, we are pulled out of line

ST. PETER'S BASILICA

and told to stand aside. Mitch comes up with the receipt of purchase for the tickets and shows it to the security guard running things. It should serve as proof of purchase. However, it is not deemed acceptable by the ticket man at the turnstile.

But he sees in her handful of documents, the correct tickets and reaches over and with a big smile, pulls them out. They are what I thought to be theater tickets! I take the blame for confusing entry tickets for promotional movie tickets. We hustle to catch up with our tour group and get headsets like everyone else for the rest of the tour.

So far this afternoon, we've been on our feet almost five hours. After we turn in our headsets to our guide, we get in another line of folks, thinking this one will go inside the great basilica. Wrong. It turns out to be a line for an elevator ride up to the base of the dome. Her Highness goes reluctantly— but then, the acrophobia kicks in. Once inside the building,

ST. PETER'S BASILICA

she is magnetically attracted to the outside wall—I mean like a mussel to a seawall. From the rail of the balcony only ten feet away, the people below at the main floor level are barely visible. The dome height is 455 feet above the interior floor and we are only halfway up. The dome of the US Capitol in DC is only 288 feet. We are at about that elevation. *This space is colossal*! I look at Mitch, and it is quite clear that this is as high as we're going to go.

Exiting the elevator back down at terra firma, we eventually find the long lines that lead into the main basilica—the one we were looking for originally. You know, the twenty-minute one.

The space inside the nave, looking up, again defies comprehension. Add the colors, the marble, the art, the gold,

ST. PETER'S BASILICA

the engineering, and most of all, the incredible design, and you have one of the absolute wonders of mankind. There is ample evidence of both genius and extreme sacrifice hanging everywhere. I stand next to a five-foot-high marble base of a giant column. It is the size of a VW Beetle; except it is perfect to the extreme. I know how to construct a car, or build a boat or an airplane, and, of course, all sorts of buildings. But I have no idea how to carve one of these bases. And not just one of them, but fifty of them—and all of them to what appears to be polished perfection. Then think about the capitals on top of the columns. That's ten times harder. All of this simply cannot be done without sacrifice and pain. The spirits are here everywhere.

The sun is inching down to its warm-color zone as we leave. I'm exhausted, but Mama Rabbit wants to see where her cell phone son, RT III, spent his architectural study-abroad semester in Rome. Using our road map, we walk a mile or two, and eventually find it. It's in a vibrant and vital urban neighborhood with sidewalk cafes and plenty of shops, markets, restaurants, and stores. And more people by the droves. Mitch will not leave until she can look at all the things she thinks her son looked at. Come on now. Give me a break!

Finally, we Uber back to the hotel in a shiny, black Mercedes van, then cross the street to a very simple, unassuming restaurant. It's almost a cafeteria. The waitress is an attractive nineteen-year-old Armenian girl who is a bundle of smiles and charm. We're the only customers, and we talk in Pidgin English. I have a plate of sliced Italian bread topped with cheese and salmon. Mitch has the house specialty, spaghetti. We each have a glass of house white and decide that tomorrow we'll go see what's going on in Pompeii.

It's only 8:30, but, properly stuffed, we go back across the street to the hotel, read for a while, and wind down.

We just finished the tour of St. Peter's Basilica and we're physically beat.

All I can say right now is that this building is a study of art, engineering, creativity, determination, sacrifice and spirituality carried beyond the imaginings of the normal mortal spirit

But, before I calm down too much, let me share a quick thumbnail sketch of my understanding of the history of this unbelievable masterpiece of architecture.

ST. PETER'S

As you've heard, Jesus died on the cross and three days later *went to heaven and sitteth on the right hand of God.* But Christianity didn't immediately blossom up all over the eastern Mediterranean area. Proselytizing was the job of the twelve Disciples Jesus left behind. It was their job to spread The Word as far and wide as possible. Simon Peter made it all the way to the mouth of the dragon—Rome—and actually stirred up an enthusiastic audience there. Of course, the Roman Empire was principally a pagan state and still viewed the followers of Jesus's teachings, like Peter, worthy of persecution; hence the public slaughter of martyrs at the hands of gladiators (or in the jaws of lions) in The Forum. Peter, an outwardly determined guy, not unlike like Jesus, was summarily crucified on a cross in Rome. This religious/cultural conflict between the Pagans and Christians went on in Rome for a couple of hundred years. As a start-up religion, it was during these tough times that Christianity was writing the verses for what would become their Holy Bible, and organizing religious objectives for the spiritual conversion of all mankind. *Tough times* is probably too soft a description for the early Christians in those days. I expect that public martyrdom was an exciting blood-sport for one side of the equation and a terrifying option for all the early Believers.

    Finally, in 306 AD, along came Constantine the Great, the first Roman Emperor to convert to Christianity. Everything changed very quickly. The Roman Empire became the *Holy* Roman Empire and the religious mood reversed itself completely. After his conversion to Christianity, Constantine, in 325 AD, ordered a new basilica built in honor of Peter the

Disciple—the man who had brought The Word to Rome—and who paid such a bitter price for it. Thirty three years later, the first St Peters Basilica was complete.

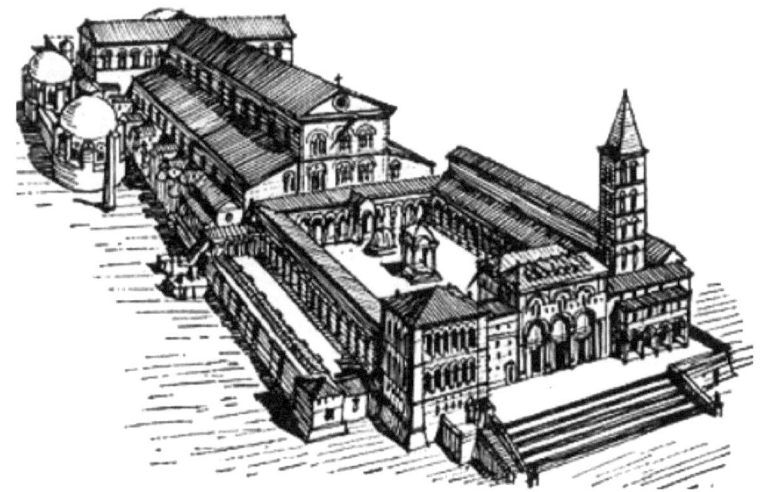

THE ORIGINAL ST PETERS BASILICA, ROME

Judging the character and scale of the attached sketch, in my opinion, it may have had a scale and character that might be more inviting than the extraordinary one just across town that we were just blown away with. But who knows?

The original St Peters' lasted over a thousand years and got Christianity through the Dark Ages, and then, in the mid-1300s, through the Black Death. Twenty million people succumbed to The Plague.

Much of Europe went silent. Islam, then expanding mostly along on the other side of the Mediterranean Sea, grew at a healthy rate territorially, culturally and scientifically. It even ruled Spain for 800 years. Finally, the Renaissance came along and Europe re-awakened with a start. By then, the old St Peters Basilica was in rough structural shape.

So in 1506, Pope Julius II decided to build the newer, bigger, better model. The first architect for the new church was Donato Bramante. He envisioned a giant Greek-cross design modeled after the Roman Pantheon. That is to say, the floor plan was basically a giant plus-sign of great halls and a huge dome covering the whole thing.

Unfortunately, Bramante died only eight years after the start of construction and a succession of nine other architects would put their thumbs in the pie. Not surprisingly, each seemed to have his own notion about what the *greatest building ever built* ought to look like, and how it would work. The floor plans changed back and forth between the Greek-cross, which has equal legs, to the more familiar Latin cross. This is the one with the large narthex projected out in front of the nave to hold a waiting congregation. Thusly, it forms the Christian Cross.

Michelangelo was the sixth architect who worked on the design. He solidified the Greek cross design but changed the single-shell dome to a double dome—one inside the other, with a void in-between the two. He felt that a simple hemispheric dome needed greater dignity, so he added the more elliptical exterior dome to enliven the visual presentation. I wonder if the hemispherical dome didn't recall the then-familiar Moorish expression of Mosque. But that is pure speculation on my part.

Interestingly, for Michelangelo, the recognition as *architect* was an easy one. His brain was already locked in a 3D mode. His sculptural masterpiece of David in Florence and the Pieta in St Peters was second nature to him.

He considered himself a sculptor, although painting was his bread and butter. And if you think painting is a tough way to make your mark, try frescos. This is a process of mixing colors in plaster and troweling onto a surface before it dries. However, yielding to pressure from his patrons, he painted the famous fresco of the finger of God about to touch the finger of Adam on the ceiling of the Sistine Chapel. Then he painted The Last Judgment on the Sanctuary wall. To this day, both are world class masterpieces without peer.

I mean, what else can you say about a guy like this?

Carlo Moderno, was the last architect on the job. Anchor man! He gets credit for adding the narthex to the Greek cross and making it a traditional Cruciform plan. Now, here we are five hundred years later and we can finally see his vision. There is absolutely no other way to handle all these tourists. Thank you, Number Ten.

Incidentally, when Moderno added the Narthex and the new front elevation, it obscures the view of the dome. This is precisely what Michelangelo didn't want to happen.

See? Nobody's perfect!

Permit me to add an aside to this aside. Leonardo DiVinci also considered his painting talent a sideline business. He carried Mona Lisa, all rolled up, around with him for years, just in case he had to show a Patron that, if he had to, he could also handle a brush and oils.

DAY 12
ROMA

Daylight Savings Time comes to Rome and breathes new life into our recently cured jetlag.

We Uber from the hotel to the train/bus station to catch the train to Naples. There is a lot of pedestrian confusion going on at the station. Because a bus might actually be quicker and easier, we go to the back side of the terminal to see if we can catch one. The cop directing traffic at the bus side of station tells us that it is much better to take the train. He's fairly emphatic, so back we go to the trains and start trying to figure it all out again. We finally do, but only because Mitch will go up to anyone and just start asking questions in English (with just a hint of a middle Tennessee accent for flavor). It works incredibly well. We load on a bullet train, the 187-mph kind, and it's again a beautiful ride.

Tunnels, however, are almost a problem. The suddenly compressed air pressure makes for serious ear popping before you can swallow. Then swoosh! You're back out again and have to unswallow to un-pop.

But the passing scenery is without fault. It just goes by too fast. Cars and trucks going in the same direction as the train are zooming backwards. All too soon, the train then unloads us in a glitzy terminal-turned-shopping-mall called Napoli Central Terminal.

Napoli: And the Fine Art of Pickpocketing

Mitch and I step off the train from Rome, and I'm sitting at a ticket machine playing what feels like electronic *slots*. The jackpot is to win two round-trip tickets from here in Naples to the ruins of Pompeii. Actually, these slots are really just automatic ticket dispensers, but the element of chance just won't go away.

After pushing the Union Jack icon for English, a woman's electronic voice comes on. She (or it) doesn't say, "Welcome to Naples." She greets you with, "Please be careful of pickpockets."

Did a vending machine really just say that to me? Come on now.

The Napoli Centrale Station brazenly touts its large-scale urbanity. Slim, European-cut business suits all seem to know where they're going. The softer-edged crowd, with strollers and baggage, stand gazing up at what look like the New York Stock Exchange *Big Boards*. Everybody is anxiously scanning rows of information for their number to hit. All the latest train data scrolls through on a ninety-second reset cycle. When fresh numbers roll over, the gathered team does a fast break in all directions, and a new team gradually assembles to take their positions for *their* numbers to roll over.

The train station itself is modern, clean, and most of all, a grand expression of contemporary metropolitan marketing. The broad hallways sparkle with glass and neon. Shop names glitter.

Under a vast architectural structure, the Ferrari-red, slant-nosed bullet trains have come to feed at the mall. They glisten and smell of ozone, and are apparently oblivious to the parasites moving up and down their flanks. They have no eyes. Every feature is glossed into smooth aerodynamic perfection. Up here in the bright lights, the Bullets rule!

The more familiar working-class trains, however, do their duty one floor below. After a ten-minute walk from our *bullet-ride* departure gate, we descend into the underbelly of the station. Down here is where the glitz meets the graffiti. The lighting is no longer crisp LED spots interrupting flowing ribbons of blue and red neon. Here, the rather cool, green-cast of fluorescent tubes compete with the hazy gray-white light coming from way down there where the railroad tracks lead to the far off mysteries of the Old World.

The trains down here don't pull in and back out like the double-ended serpents upstairs. Here, they mechanically brake to a stop, exhale compressed air from their braking systems, mindlessly drop off a spent batch of commerce, and take on another load.

But don't get me wrong. This is not Dante's *Inferno* down here. It's just that the contrast with the sparkle and twinkle upstairs emphasizes the utility aspect of people-hauling in and out of the basement.

Down here, there are no handsome and dispassionate security guards with cocky berets, combat boots, and automatic weapons slung on the ready across their chest. Down here, we're just working folks waiting for the local.

The assigned track for Pompeii is right at the foot of the ramp coming down from upstairs. The route map on the wall shows about twenty stops to our destination, and the timetable indicates the trip will take a shade over an hour. The next train is due in twenty minutes. We just missed the last train, so we easily find two seats on a bench. It even has a back to relax against. We're facing the empty track. Incrementally, the crowd begins to build. We spend our time reading up on the history of Pompeii. We're comfortable, and everything is going well.

Unbeknownst to us, of course, somewhere in this gathering group of travelers are at least three sets of eyes making a judgment concerning their morning's livelihood. There is a couple of yards space between our bench and the yellow-and-black caution stripes on the edge of the platform. So, right now, the appraising eyes are either behind us, looking at our white hair, or off to the side, assessing their prey. I'm wearing jeans and a gray sport coat. Mitch has on black slacks and a comfortably fitting, light-beige, woolen jacket with a wide, black leather-like waist belt. I like her outfit because it makes her easy to spot in a crowd of the uniformly dark European attire.

It's impossible to say where the bad guys pick up our trail. After we sat down, maybe they walked up behind us to confirm that we were speaking English. But that really isn't necessary. To the trained eye, there is no hiding *tourist*.

In retrospect, looking at the forthcoming little caper from the perp's point of view, I would like to think that our energy level and physical dexterity would have deterred them. But, of course, it did not. As we will see, their tactics will work on the fleet of foot, the quick of mind, or the swift of hand.

Our train finally rolls into the station, slows to a stop, beeps its plaintive horn, opens its doors, and disgorges its cargo. The already packed platform is immediately double-packed with people going in the opposite direction. After the bulk of discharged passengers finally filter through, momentum shifts to our team, *the boarding-crowd*. We start hurry-shuffling toward the door openings between the cars. Mitch, slightly ahead of me, gets into the transition space first. This area is small, about nine feet square. From there, she flows with the crowd directly through the single door to the car to the left. I'm caught up in a little confusion of some people trying to decide which car to enter, the one to the left or the right. There may also be somebody still trying to get off.

Then a big guy, probably my size (but half as old), stops halfway in the doorwway to the left and holds on to a grab bar bolted to the ceiling of the train. He's got it gripped with both hands and is immovable. The rest of the passengers have to squirm around him or go to the car to the right. It's his fixedness that is causing a traffic jam. I think he's stopped there because maybe he wants get back off at the next stop. There is an eager somebody behind me pushing me aside so that he can get around the big guy. Then there is another man at my left side and a little ahead, who slows down, and stops, then pushes me back a little. He turns around to face me and shifts like he wants to go to the car to the right. If this sounds confusing, it's because it is. And to add to the mix, everybody is rattling off Italian like soccer moms at a little league game. A growing sense of conflict slowly starts triggering dormant adrenaline glands.

But my goal is simple. I am concerned about getting into the same car with Nancy.

Incrementally, the shoving gets a little more aggressive than it needs to be. Then I've had enough of it. I plant my feet and turn to confront the guy behind me. This shoving business is going to come to an end—right now—language barrier or not!

Timed perfectly, a beep-beep-beep-warning goes off, and the exterior door of the train starts to slide closed. The three guys move as one toward the door. The closest guy jambs his foot in the doorsill when it is halfway closed. The door recycles to the full-open position, and the three of them whisk briskly through. They then walk directly to a set of dark stairs going up that I had not noticed previously. Before they are halfway to the stair, the train door has closed normally. The beeping ceases, and that quick, they're gone, and the train is buttoned up and headed south.

As we pick up speed I'm thinking: *Obviously, those dopes must have gotten on the wrong train. No wonder they were so confused.*

With the sudden release of confrontational pressure, I start to replay this event in my mind. *Something's not right about all this—too much happened too fast.* Confused people are seldom so assertive in their actions. Confusion suggests uncertainty. There was no uncertainty about those three fellows wanting to exit this train—and right now!

Just on an outside chance, a curiosity really, I reach down into the left front pocket of my blue jeans; the one I keep my money clip in. The pocket is empty!

I can't believe it!

With quick apprehension, I then reach for my right rear pocket, the one I keep my small credit card wallet in. It is still there. I hold my breath while I reach in my inside jacket pocket for my passport.

It is there. It was only my cash that was stolen.

Still left standing in this little vestibule are two men in dark work clothes and a middle-aged woman leaning back on the handrail. All three of them just look at me. Their hapless, blank expressions tell me *they know*.

I ask in English, "Did you see what just happened?"

None of them answers, but each one then looks away. They understood me. But then, almost orchestrated, all three file into the car opposite the one Mitch is in. (Now, as I type all this up, I wonder if they might have been field judges.)

I go through the door to Mitch's car and move up as close as I can to get to earshot distance. She got the last seat in the car and there are a dozen people already standing in the isle with me.

In a stage whisper of just two sentences, I tell her. "Mitch, I have just been pickpocketed. Are you okay?"

She has her purse in her hands and says, almost with a smile, "I'm fine."

AD LIB

A trim, young woman, probably thirty-five or forty, in a gray business suit and rimless glasses, with inquisitive auburn eyes, maybe a school teacher, looks at me and asks, "Pickpocket?"

Everyone around us then looks over at me.

I answer. "Si. Pickpocket."

A guy standing next to the auburn eyes' woman rubs his thumb against his forefinger with the international signal for "how much?"

I raise two fingers.

He asks, "Mille?"

Local expectation of what American tourists carry as pocket money must be pretty high.

The ball's back in my court. I answer, "No. Dos cento."

I don't know if that is correct Italian for two hundred. It may not even be proper Spanish, but it's close to *centum* in Latin. The guy rolls his eyes, raises his eyebrows and shrugs one shoulder like, "*Oh well. That's not so bad.*"

The facial expressions here are all in Italian. But as Leonardo da Vinci taught the whole world, facial languages don't need translators.

Just as you would expect, when the dust settles, my emotions start to rise. My sense of personal violation far exceeds the loss in cash. I have a feeling that I would like to replay the whole incident, but this time I'd show those thugs a thing or two. This reaction is probably called something like male PMR—Post-Macho-Remorse.

Mitch's reaction is very interesting. She just kind of backs away from it; like it is my problem and I need to figure it out. She's obviously interested, but never does she appraise my reaction, or overreaction. She simply backs off a little bit and lets time take its course.

Reviewing this incident, as I am doing now without the heat-of-the-moment emotions, suggests that the consequences of what just occurred could have made a far more thrilling story than the loss of a couple hundred euros ($250).

The real questions are how serious were these robbers? Were they armed, and in the event of serious confrontation, did they have an alternate strategy? How combative were they prepared to be to protect their illicit trade? Do they have a plan B of three karate chops, mace in the face and they are gone? Or is it a single 9-mm hole in the chest?

Obviously, I have absolutely no way of knowing the answers to any of this. But the indications are that these pickpockets were a well-practiced team. Their skill, however, does not preclude me from appreciating artisan craft choreographed by an efficient and well trained troupe. For a country as fine and respected as Italy, this conduct, which appears be well known, is a pity.

As I suggest, these guys here in Naples are highly skilled in their enterprise. So, one must ask, *Is what I have described here their only game plan?* I would guess not. I have a suspicion that the Big Guy is the leader. This guess is only because he can see everything. The three of them go into a terminal at a predetermined time that has been calculated from fundamental rush hour experience. That part's easy. The Boss picks a Target and gives hand signals like a third-base coach does when he pulls his left ear or brushes fleas off his shirt sleeve. But, again, this is only conjecture. They may be more sophisticated than that and use earbuds. Or they may be like trained actors and can play every heist from intuition. Or, maybe, when they spotted Nancy and me, the Boss says, "Okay guys. This is a 3B with a half-door, JATO assist, stair two. Start the count when I reach up for the grab bar. Star burst at seven. Take positions." (Don't try to figure that out. I just made it up.)

I trust that sharing this short narrative will alert you to some of the excitement going on in foreign travel. And if you're lucky, you might have a daughter like mine who will give you a money belt a month before your baptism by fire. My belt came with a cautious admonition, "Now, Dad. I know you don't need this and probably won't wear it, but you might think about it."

As it turned out, I did think about it, and I did have it on during this heist. And it did have enough greenbacks in it to permit Nancy and me to walk into any airport in Europe and buy two plane tickets, on the spot, to Atlanta. It also had a spare high-limit credit card, photocopies of our passports and a photocopy of our return ticket on Delta, Paris—Atlanta.

So do I recommend that everyone wear a money belt?

Of course not. But for those of us without much experience in foreign travel, and those of us burdened with a visceral need for self-reliance, it works. Am I overcautious? Sure. But it's out of inexperience with the system. Not fear.

Like any good experience, this trip had a number of lessons. One of the big items is that the economic system in Europe blends very nicely with what we're used to here in the

States. Just a good credit card or two makes it remarkably seamless. Another is the cell phone. If we should need to make a call home for help, it's as quick as it is when we're walking down Peachtree Street.

So, when Mitch and I come back here again, will I still wear a money belt? Probably. But this time, not to hoard cash. Until I learn otherwise, I will carry a spare credit card and a photocopy of our passport IDs. Sorry, but that's just me being me. Old habits, you know.

Oh, yes. If you haven't been there, don't miss Pompeii. It still smells of the rich Roman culture from when Vesuvius blew her top in AD 79.

When Mitch and I were exiting the amphitheater and heading back to catch the local trainback to Naples, I

THE TRANSITION SPACE BETWEEN CARS WHERE THIS EVENT OCCURRED

wondered if this very arena was where the first-generation pickpocket perfected the ***three-man press***.

But obviously it couldn't have been—togas don't have pockets.

Sorry. I got caught up in all that pickpocket stuff, but I'm back on subject now.

The Pompeii Train Station is only two hundred yards from the entrance to the 140-acre restoration site. For those of us waiting to get entry tickets, there is a long line that doubles back on itself twice. It takes forty-five minutes to get our tickets but we're finally ready to start the program—except we haven't had a bite to eat since last night. All the restaurants in the park have been closed down since Vesuvius blew. So back outside the gate we find a couple of comfortable seats

DOWNTOWN POMPEII

in an open-air sidewalk café. Hanging above us are trees and trellises, song birds chirping, and blooming flowers. Ahh! We then enjoy some kind of vegetable-and-cheese sandwiches, and each of us has another one of those incredible Coke Cola's. Back home, neither one of us is really a Coke drinker. But when one is good, it has no peer.

Once refueled, we're anxious to get started, so we head straight to the forum in the center of the ancient city. As we're walking, trying not to trip over the giant roadbed boulders, Mitch is still reading up on the history of this once thriving metropolis.

The entire excavation is another sterling example of intellectual/historical/cultural/social/political/architectural

A WORKING MAN'S COLUMN, POMPEII (CAN'T AFFORD MARBLE? MAKE IT OUT OF TILE.)

overload. After thirty minutes of trying to absorb everything at once, cerebral filters clog and the brain clutch freewheels without traction. The mental transmission starts to smoke. "Look at that bath. Look at these columns. Look at that kitchen. Come here and look at this…"

There is a sense that the lost civilization has just recently vacated the premises. For fear that we will miss something, we walk straight to the very farthest point of the site. From there, we will work our way back to the entrance. We're both tired and running on nervous energy. Now is not the time to slow down. Three hours of continuous in-and-out of ruins is a fair piece of work.

NOTICE THE DEEP CART-TRACK GROOVES IN THE PAVING.

THE POMPEII COLOSSEUM

It's three p.m. and, finished here or not, we need to head back to the station. Once we get there, a train is just departing. We wait until 3:40 for the next one. Our high-speed train reservations from Naples to Rome are for 5:10. Again, I get a little nervous about the time. But I tell myself, "Relax. If we miss the train, we may lose sixty dollars, or maybe it's redeemable. In any event, it's just a missed train. And missed trains offer more unanticipated opportunities than caught trains every time. Besides, there's always another train going somewhere. And don't forget, dummy. You just lost four times that much money by letting yourself get pickpocketed."

I'm not letting myself off that hook just yet.

But the schedule works out the boring way (i.e., we catch the train to Naples and walk over to the fiery red serpent headed to Rome). The Italians call this fast one, Frecciarossa. It is as fast and smooth as ever.

At 200 kph, Mitch and I both marvel at the fertility of the landscape whizzing by. Much of it is still deeply scarred by quarries of either limestone, marble, or gravel used to build the Eternal City.

We ease to a silent stop at the Rome station and Uber to the hotel. Cost—twenty-five dollars! This is a total rip-off! A taxi would be half that much. I just pay it and tell Mitch we're going to go have a nice dinner and not get pulled into a confrontation about anything. She's fine with that, and we eat at the same restaurant where we supped yesterday.

Tonight, at the three tables next to us, a family party of fifteen is having a great evening together. I have my second glass of wine in Italy. It's a pleasure to share the fun of spooling down with Mitch. Everything has been butter smooth between us. A glass of wine can be a small but rewarding ceremony. The evening of assimilating the experiences of today is welcome.

DAY 13

ROME TO FLORENCE

Last night, on hotels.com, I booked rooms in Florence for tonight and in Venice for tomorrow night. The Bnb in Florence costs seventy-five dollars, and I forgot to write down the cost of the hotel in Venice. Seems like it was expensive, maybe about $250.

This morning we catch what I think is a Frecciarossa to Florence at 8:50 a.m., but it turns out to be a workaday semi-express. This is perfectly fine. The weather is again gorgeous, and sitting in a commuter train with a bunch of people going to work is comfortable and friendly.

I spend half of the trip working on this journal. For me, this chore is both personally enjoyable and intellectually essential. In a way, it's like creating architecture. Ideas are incredibly important, but it takes brick and mortar to make

them permanent. Look at the picture of what I called the "Working Man's Column" in Pompeii and you'll see what I mean. The idea of pie-piece brick column was simply a good idea in some guy's head until he sat down and built it. Now, two thousand years later, no matter how humble his talent, the physical evidence of his creativity still exists. Perhaps the same holds true for the written word. Who knows? (Or ask Socrates)

From the Florence train station, we catch a taxi to the Hotel Costini, one block from the great and iconic Duomo cathedral.

The hotel lobby is accessed via a three-story elevator ride in a wire-walled, three-foot-by-three-foot cab that runs up and down between the square set of stairs. The construction is similar to the Bnb in Rome. It's still too early to move in our room, so we just check in and dump our two suitcases in a space behind the desk. We wiggle back into the cage and go down and out through the iron-gated door that opens almost secretly onto the people-packed street. Elegant, this joint ain't. But clean, centrally located, and satisfactory, it is. We then stroll over to the Duomo like we were guests at the Ritz.

The ticket line moves briskly and takes only thirty minutes. The tour takes another forty-five. Without question, the cathedral is large and impressive to the extreme. But because it is pre-Gothic, it doesn't have all the glass and sparkle we've gotten used to—or I should say, spoiled by. The exterior walls are thick, bearing monoliths of elegant white-and-green marble. There are but a few windows and

BATTISTERO SAN GIOVANNI, FLORENCE

little stained glass. Flying buttresses and cantilevered gargoyles are waiting for future generations to invent. The mood is sober and somber as opposed to dazzling and enlightened. Perhaps, here, the spirit swells rather than soars. Everything has its place.

Next comes the hike up to the Galleria Accademia to see Michelangelo's statue of David. Guess what? Closed on Mondays. No problem. There is replica David, full size, which stands equally proud over by the river at the Palazzo Vecchio. The substitute was placed there when the real David got indoor accommodations at the Accademia in 1910.

Once there, I take a classic shot of Mitch with David on her shoulder. We then head to the Ponte Vecchio Bridge

THE DUOMO, FLORENCE

and take a jillion more pictures. You can't help it. Then it's up to the Palazzo Pitti (Pitti Palace), but they're closed, too. So we head over to the Romanesque-Gothic St. Mary del Carmine Church, and they're also closed!

THE DUOMO, FLORENCE

Obviously, that's about all we can see of medieval Florence for today, so we head back to check into the hotel. So far we've walked five and a half miles today.

After an hour's rest and a little pleasure reading, but without a nap, we head out for dinner. On the perimeter of an intricately patterned local square, there's a busy little restaurant with lots of plate glass overlooking the plaza. Some American guy, maybe the same guy from Paris, with a guitar and a very loud suitcase-speaker system, is singing Bolare-style music. The musical presentation is nothing like the locals we saw a couple of days ago in the train station in Rome. There, one guy was playing the daylights out of an upright piano with his buddy singing opera arias *con gusto*! If they were not professionals, they should have been. But no one is complaining about music either great or small, here or there. To our ears, it's all welcome background mood-streaming.

We're seated not at a window, but next to the kitchen. I'm served a deliciously prepared lasagna and Mitch a mountainous salad. *Overfull and really tired* is a peasant's blessing. Maybe the very best there is. Thank you, Florence.

Ten p.m. and we crash.

Rome to Florence

DAY 14

Florence to Venice

Despite the fact that there was construction noise down the hall last night, and chairs were dragged over tile floors above us, and there were also some voices coming through the ventilation system, eventually it got quiet and dark and we enjoyed a good night's sleep.

Breakfast (coffee, cereal, and rolls) cost an extra four dollars at the Bnb. We flag a taxi to the train station (eight dollars), but as it turns out, the train to Venice is a no-bullet ride either. And again, this is just fine. No, in fact, it is preferable. It feels more like handmade lasagna than fast food.

The ride takes two and a half hours. We're pretty comfortable just sitting here for a while watching Italy go by at something like a comprehensible speed. I think this proves Einstein's Theory of Relativity unequivocally: time slows down as velocity increases. Here it is. Proof-positive, right before our eyes!

The train station in Venice is a bustle of activity. The time-warp just sped up again.

Conveniently, the train terminal abuts the Grand Canal. And it's just a short block to buy water-bus tickets. We load our bags on a fairly crowded boat and start the first leg of an eight stop trip to San Marco Piazza. The warp just slowed down again. Obviously the chamber of commerce arranged to dump tourists a couple of blocks short of the big square so that they (we) can shop all the stores and curio markets along the way.

We postpone the commercial challenge and eventually find the Hotel Antico Panada. It's located just a few blocks down a seven-foot-wide passageway from San Marco. The lobby is tiny, but very classy. Mirrors, artwork, and crystal

chandeliers almost clutter the space. We check into room 222, and the quality of the interior design is even nicer than the lush lobby. There is an oversized, Venetian crystal chandelier in our room and the walls are padded with three-quarter-inch upholstered fabric that feels uncommonly elegant. The two windows in the corner of the room have outside shutters and inside drapes and curtains. With the

PIAZZA SAN MARCO

casements open, I can almost reach the open casements of the building across the little side alley.

After unpacking, we walk back to San Marco, then off into the side streets to go exploring. I make note of gondola docks for future use. Window shopping is enjoyable, but eventually our energy flags and we stop to eat at a sidewalk café. I have fettuccini with shrimp and whiskey. The whiskey part is illusionary to make the fettuccini sound better. I think it works. Mitch has a salad, and we share our meals fifty-fifty. It is a simple but gratifying dinner, and a glass of house white makes it feel a little classier. We turn in at ten.

DAY 15
VENICE

We're up at 8:00 and have breakfast in the hotel dining room. Our first mission today is to locate the Guggenheim Museum. Mitch finds the number icon for museums on the city map she got from the front desk and steers us about a mile through narrow passageways and over a dozen bridges and canals to get there. The labyrinth of pedestrian walkways boggles the mind. Keep in mind that there are neither cars nor bicycles in Venice. It's boats and feet, and that's it.

Our destination turns out to be not the Guggenheim Museum, but a very attractive little church. My guide picked the wrong number four. The blue number four is for churches, and the red number four is for museums. The graphic designer of this map must have been new to the trade.

It turns out that the G-Museum is now two miles south of us. Rather than backtracking, Mitch picks a better way to travel—the water bus. We find a station/dock and pay ten dollars each and have another little adventure. It is an interesting, elegant, and wonderful boat ride through the city. The wind has picked up, and there is a little taste of blowing, brackish spray—just barely enough to enjoy. This is why you *make it up as you go along.*

We tour the museum, which is chock-full of Picasso's, Klee's, Pollock's—all the big-name stuff. After two hours, we then walk back to the boat station and catch a water taxi a quarter mile across the Grand Canal to San Marco to meet Holden at the Campanile.

Today is the first time that Mitch and I have had time to spend with Holden when not in the company of his parents. This is a treat. Remember: he's the twenty-year-old son of my Little Brother, Damon. Damon and I are products of the Big Brothers/Big Sisters organization. We were matched up two or three years before Mitch and I were married, so he's always been family. Holden is now on a study-abroad program with Tulane University. How proud do you think I am to make this second-generation connection in Venice, Italy?

I try not to, but I can't help but study Holden closely. There is evidence of the reserved dignity of his father's brilliant and classical mind at work. There is also the electric personality of his outgoing and energetic mother. Both parents are architects of notable accomplishments. Holden never had a chance but to be exceptional on so many levels. And then he's handsome to boot! Sometimes life just ain't fair to the rest of us.

Venice

However, for Mitch and me, we now have the consolidation of two of our dearest family/friends into one bright and personable young man—and he knows the city.

The three of us walk around the corner from our hotel to an open piazza for lunch. We sit and talk for an hour and a half while eager pigeons land bullishly on our table to share the pizza crusts.

Tiring of the bird hassle, we then hike over to a gondola rental dock. A forty-minute ride costs one hundred dollars. Wow! But for me, this is a necessity. It brands Holden and Venice into the trip. It's also the sister cruise to the chilly sightseeing-boat ride on the Seine last week.

The gondolier points out Amadeus Mozart's house along the way. Interestingly, the gondoliers aren't allowed to sing anymore. It would make them entertainers and that would involve a whole different union. The slow, quiet, restful

HOLDEN HOLDIN' FORTH

interlude of the ride adds its own unique dimension to Venice. Expensive and hokey is excusable once in a while, isn't it?

With the helping hand of the happy gondolier, we carefully climb out of the black-lacquered boat. Actually it isn't nearly as tippy as it looks.

We then sign up for a two-hour *tour d'foot* of the Doge's Palace. Talk about a big, elegant, and sort of a rundown museum. This is it. The art, heraldry, and suits of armor of the 1300s are worthy of plenty of consideration. And there is a lot of wonderful stuff to look at. But the building itself shows signs of more than casual neglect. It needs rescuing.

Leaving there, we walk north a short mile through the Venetian labyrinth of alleys and canals to the Venice Hospital. This is a converted church/convent complex with dozens of fat, lazy cats lounging in all the courtyards, garden walls and tree limbs. The three of us sit on park benches under a couple of the very few trees in Venice and gossip for an hour like old fishmongers' wives. The quiet interlude becomes the highlight of a very special visit. We can't quite get enough of this just sitting and talking thing.

It's 6:00 p.m. and time to find another outdoor café on one of the many intimate interior urban piazzas close to San Marco. We order a light dinner of pizza and sliced tomatoes. Pigeons again swoop down directly onto our table to scavenge food. We share the table with them until 7:30 when we have to make our way back through the fascinating warren of passageways to our hotel. There, reluctantly, we say goodnight to Holden. What an impressive young man. He's flying to Marrakesh, Morocco, tomorrow morning to see a friend; we have a very early flight to Paris.

Venice

I'm sitting in the hotel room this evening while Mitch is out shopping for knickknacks to take home. Apparently, she just remembered she still has family back in America.

If it is true that architecture is the spiritual union of art, tradition, culture and technology, then Venice has got to be one of its cornerstones. The first three of these qualities are evident everywhere here—from the gondoliers' striped shirts and straw hats with a red ribbon, to the tightly controlled Venetian Gothic architectural style you see everywhere.

Just look at the picture of San Marco Piazza below. The plaza and buildings are not built on solid earth. It's all constructed on a grid of wood pilings that have petrified into a stone-pier foundation system.

To my eye, if there is a flaw in this set-up, it's the fact that there is not a flaw anywhere. But the city is not paper-thin

SAN MARCO AT 5:30 A.M.

like a movie stage-set. It is authentic and robust in its livelihood (tourism) and letter-perfect in its execution.

On the other hand, incredible technology is everywhere, but not universally recognized.

Venice is a city built in a very large lagoon sheltered by a long string of barrier islands that protect it from the Adriatic Sea. There are three large inlets in the barrier that permit the open sea (and ocean shipping) to flow in and out freely. Hence, sea-level changes, storm surges or tidal movements are felt in the canals of Venice. In 1966, the canals overflowed to the point of having six feet of water in the Piazza San Marco. Lesser flooding occurs with frequency. To moderate the surge of tidal and/or storm flow events, the Ministry of Public Works, in 1975, initiated work on constructing flood gates in the three inlets. The project is supposed to be finished in 2022 at a cost of 8 billion dollars. Cross your fingers.

More interesting, to me at least, is the wooden pier foundation construction. Apparently, some five hundred years ago, the local folks observed that if they drove sixty foot long Oak piers deep-down through the silty bottom of the lagoon and into the hard clay below, so long as they were not exposed to the atmosphere, the piers would petrify into a stone-like hardness. To build the city, millions of such piers were place on what look like about three foot centers. They were then capped with horizontal wooden members forming underwater petrified beams. On top of the beams, a double course of stone was laid. Then, in the old tried and true masonry manner, the buildings or plazas were constructed. So, does all this engineering work perfectly?

Venice

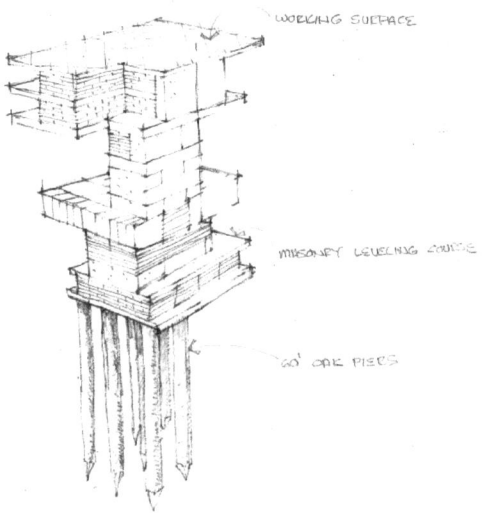

VENICE FOUNDATION SCHEMATIC

Not quite. The footprint of the city has dropped 9 inches in the last 100 years. Personally, I think some of it is because of people load.

Electrical service, telephone lines, domestic water and other utilities were then laced throughout the city at the plaza level using the hundreds of foot bridges as a path for their distribution system.

All of this ingenuity is wonderful stuff until you get to the sanitary sewer system. Guess what? Much of the waste gets dumped into the canals and flows out to sea.

Well, nothing is perfect. Adequate, sewerage treatment programs notwithstanding, Venice still remains one of the romantic wonders of the world.

DAY 16
VENICE TO PARIS

Sleep, last night, for me at least, was illusive. At midnight, I was wide awake and concerned about the schedule to take the water bus to the airport. I woke Mitch up to ask if she knew what time the water busses got going. She didn't, but agreed with my concern. We both got dressed and went down to the front desk to get better info. The clerk, a very nice-looking, enthusiastic guy, spoke excellent English and knew by heart the exact timetable for everything, including the water bus. He said we were in good shape and gave us the boost in confidence we (I) needed. I was also concerned about how to get from the water bus to the airport on the mainland. He said that was easy; you just step out of the boat and take the moving sidewalk. The water-bus dock is right at the air terminal; just like the train terminal is at another water-bus dock. All three modes of transportation simply flow into one another. Just plug and play!

We went back up to 222, and Mitch went back to sleep immediately. I set two alarms and lay there chastising myself for waking her up to do something I could have and should have done by myself. Funny, the things we worry about.

At 5:45, both of our phones go off simultaneously. Mitch bounds out of bed. I'm dragging. We check out at the front desk and walk in the predawn darkness across San Marco Piazza to the blue-line water-bus station. There, we meet another old couple, probably in their sixties. They're very nice Brits, and we chat merrily away. I am finally convinced that we are at the right station at the right time. Things are looking up.

VENICE GREETS A NEW DAY

In thirty minutes, the boat-taxi greets the dock with a resounding thump. The captain will repeat this aggressive docking technique at all of the next fifteen stops. The entire trip will take an hour. In the boat, all the passengers sit so low in the forward hold that they have to stand tippy toe to get any view through the high windows. Talk about baggage-class accommodations. The attached sunrise picture was taken through the captain's window. Fortunately, he doesn't have windshield wipers.

Finally, at the airport dock, we make our final bump-crash in the slip. Fifteen of us pile out and take a series of moving sidewalks about a quarter of a mile, right into the lobby of the new air terminal. A little apprehensively still, Mitch and I take on a computer boarding-pass machine. This time, we score on the first try. We still have ninety minutes before departure, so we order coffee and croissants at a carryout bar and find two comfortable seats to wait for the world to catch up with us.

Upon boarding, the ticket agent will not accept my carry-on luggage because it is two centimeters too long. That's three-quarters of an inch. So she checks it in as baggage. This is bologna! But there is no sense in letting it upset the beautiful morning. Checking a bag will just offer me a second chance to find Baggage Claim at Charles de Gaulle airport. I mean, how much fun can you have at CDG?

Mitch offers me her window seat. The flight over the snow-covered Alps is astonishing. Just look at that picture. It really makes you want to be down there, be a part of it, and go exploring. It's still winter in the mountains. As you can see, the general weather over this part of Europe is holding severe-clear. From this altitude, we can see the Alps of France, Switzerland, Germany, Austria, and Italy, all in one window port.

We land and in ten minutes retrieve my bag from baggage claim and catch a train to St. Michael/Notre-Dame station. Then it's only the easy walk over to our old hotel. It feels good to be back to these comfortable environs.

While Nancy primps, I set Siri for a four-minute power nap. Four minutes is my personal shortest. But if it works, it's the most efficient. I put my feet up and almost immediate black out. Siri rings. I'm awake with a sweet taste in my mouth and zero grogginess.

Mitch finishes her primp, I'm recharged, and we then walk a mile or so over to Pompidou Center. The building is now wrapped with giant panels of canvas. Perhaps it's protection for a renovation job. The exposed structure and mechanical equipment is still a marvel of architectural creativity.

Tomorrow, we're headed back home, so it's finally time to slow down. At a strolling pace, we window-shop and stop by a couple of impulse/tourist shops to pick up gifts for everybody. The long walk back to the hotel is rewarded with a tasty dinner of pizza and salad at the friendly pizzeria next to our hotel.

We're back at L'Abby at 9:00 p.m.

THOSE ARE NOT CLOUDS.
THEY ARE THE SNOW-COVERED ALPS.

THE REAR FAÇADE OF POMPIDOU CENTER

DAY 17

Paris to Atlanta

Last night I set my cell phone to ring at 6:15. Naturally, I can't sleep after 4:30. At 6:20 I'm showered and packed. Mitch is also awake, so we're off to an early start. Yesterday, so that we would have several options this morning, I bought train tickets to the airport. My thinking was that this is our last opportunity to use the Metro system. The backup method to get to the airport is to simply call a taxi—expensive but mindless. And the third is to Uber there—equally mindless, but a little less expensive (maybe).

When I check the Uber app on my phone this morning, I get no images for close-by cars. This seems strange, but it kicks them out of contention.

Next option is to take the train. We've got time, but I'm simply not ready to take on another learning process this morning. That leaves us with a taxi.

Down at the front desk, I ask the concierge to call us a cab. The sun's not up yet, and I'm already tired of thinking. Without a word, Mitch goes to the front desk and, once again, picks up the room tab ($300). Again, she has been more than generous in sharing expenses all along the trip. By the way, she and I keep our own checkbooks and credit cards. We have no joint accounts.

There is no time for breakfast, so we hop into a shiny, black Mercedes limo, and off we go. It is still three hours before our departure time. The airport is less than an hour away, and I feel comfortable about our timing. It's time to relax a little.

But as it turns out, Paris really does have a rush hour traffic issue. It's not so evident downtown, but when we start inching out to the burbs, it starts to feel like Atlanta; except here, there are a zillion motorcycles that weave in and out of every lane of opportunity. The motor bikes are constantly searching for hidden fissures in the flow. But horns don't blow. If traffic starts to thin out, then along comes another gaggle of motorcycles and scooters to fill the void.

I start to get nervous about time again. Thankfully, watching the two-wheel traffic compete for position takes my mind off my wrist watch. All of us—cars, trucks, motorcycles, and bicycles—weave and dance with reckless abandon. The trip, however, only takes a little over an hour and costs eighty-five dollars. But, most important of all, we're back on schedule.

At the hotel, thinking we would enjoy a leisurely breakfast at the airport, we skipped some pretty nice fixings already laid out. That decision may have saved our bacon, because after we get our boarding passes from the vending machine, we go to the luggage-check counter. This operation is an incompetent mess and takes over a half an hour to shuffle through. Then, as we walk up to the entrance to the security gate, we are confronted with a *four-hundred-person line*! Apparently, airport security is on *high alert*, and they are pre-checking passports *before* entry into the terminal proper. There is no accordion effect. The line isn't shuffling, not even a little bit. It looks inert. This is going to screw up *any* departure time today.

There is no question now that we are going to have difficulty making our flight. We still have the *real* security check-in to go through, and we have not yet caught the commuter train to the correct gate. It is now 10:15. Our departure time is 10:20. For some reason Mitch seems perfectly at peace with the problem. She and I are now on completely different wavelengths concerning the need to hustle to make the flight. I'm hoping that because of the extra security alert, they'll hold the flight a few minutes.

We eventually get through the passport-check line to then go through Security. This line is fairly efficient, but it's still a distance to where we pick up the shuttle to our terminal gate.

We catch the shuttle at 10:25.

Damnation! We've obviously missed the flight now by five minutes. But you never know. There is no choice but to keep pressing. I keep hanging on to the notion that all flights may be held up ten minutes. It's our only hope.

The shuttle train takes us to terminal M, but our gate is M50. Yes, that's the twenty-fifth station on the right, down at the end of the great concourse. Mitch is still just walking. Not only is she lagging behind, but now she's talking to another woman who is also in no great hurry! I'm speed-walking ahead—and starting to fume a little.

Way up there, it looks like a quarter of a mile, I think I can see a few people standing at the last gate, M50. I pick up my pace to a quasi-jog while pulling one piece of luggage in each hand. Their four wheels are clicking like playing cards in bicycle spokes. If I can get there before the gate closes, I'll prevail. I *will* keep the door open until Her Highness and her chatty, new best friend finally elect to make their elegant appearance.

But I can't wait. I pick up my pace to a trot.

And about out of breath, I finally make it there, and the gate is still wide open!

It takes me three giant steps to finally slow down. I'm breathing heavily.

The sign above the gate says the flight is scheduled to take off at 10:45. My twenty-eight-dollar, accurate-to-a-second Timex says it's now 10:29.

Well guess what? My eagerness caused just another early arrival. So what's new about that?

This is the second time in two weeks that I have erred in mentally recording a train schedule. Hmm—might be something to think about. But what did Scarlett say? "Fiddle de dee, I'll worry about that tomorrow."

Mitch, as she always does, finally arrives in her own time and just smiles. She holds the tickets and knew all along that she would eventually make it on time. Again, she patiently tolerates my error and impulsiveness. I wonder if she just lets me blow steam only because it's easier than trying to turn an old battlewagon.

We're now at altitude, west-bound over the Mid-Atlantic; bone-tired, still friends, and patiently digesting Delta's tourist class, efficiently served, airline lunch.

Just so there is no question about it, we are also completely satisfied with ourselves and enjoying the spent afterglow of an experience in full. Plus, we are both looking forward to getting back to the comfort of the old *coming and going—buying and selling, early and late*. Remember all that, Milton?

The glow in the plane—that thin luminous mist that only we can see—comes from our returning home with a little different perspective of life than the one we left with. And that difference is not generated so much by *what* we saw in Europe—but by *how* we saw it.

If I succeed in sharing this *how-you-see-it* notion, then the visit to the gilded gates of Versailles and the ride in the glossy-black gondola on the Grand Canal is not really what this journal is all about. The pictures and stories I've presented here are only the stage set to life's never-ending, always changing, sitcom skit about people.

As you might guess, much like experimental sex, the ad lib approach to life is not for everyone. In fact (and again like ES), many very nice people will be completely turned off by it. However, those folks are still entitled to ask the question, *Why would anyone purposefully introduce the opportunity for discomfort, uncertainty or disappointment, unless that is precisely what they are seeking? And seeking uncertainty doesn't make any sense at all!*

The response is easy. *If your comfort zone is defined by maintaining minimum risk, then that's the way you ought to play-out your life.* Said another way, avoiding risk ain't wrong—not even by a little bit.

And there is the argument: *There is risk in every first kiss. That's why it's so good, isn't it?*

But, enough of that. My purpose, in this journal, is to share an alternative approach (i.e., what it's like to take a two week, *unplanned* trip around Europe—just to see what happens when you make it up as you go along).

One more time: it's not what you see. *It's how you see it* that creates the enduring memories. The rest is just JPG imagery..

Thank you for coming along. Please forgive my imperfections and personal foibles I've so bountifully shared. It's been a fun ride.

A JOURNALIST'S COVE

www.ingramcontent.com/pod-product-compliance
Lightning Source LLC
Chambersburg PA
CBHW041503010526
44118CB00001B/5